Lands

Easte... n
CRETE

a countryside guide
Sixth edition

Jonnie Godfrey
and
Elizabeth Karslake
revised by Sunflower Books

Sixth edition © 2023
Sunflower Books™
PO Box 36160
London SW7 3WS, UK
www.sunflowerbooks.co.uk

ISBN 978-1-85691-547-2

Colours of Crete

Important note to the reader

We have done our best to ensure that the descriptions and maps in this book are error-free at press date. The book will be updated, where necessary, in future editions. It is always very helpful for us to receive your comments (sent in care of info@sunflowerbooks.co.uk, please) for the updating of future editions.

We also rely on those who use this book — especially walkers — to take along a good supply of common sense when they explore. Conditions change fairly rapidly on Crete, and *storm damage or bulldozing may make a route unsafe at any time*. If the route is not as we outline it here, and your way ahead is not secure, return to the point of departure. *Never attempt to complete a tour or walk under hazardous conditions!* Please read carefully the notes on pages 46-54, as well as the introductory comments at the beginning of each tour and walk (regarding road conditions, equipment, grade, distances and time, etc). Explore *safely*, while at the same time respecting the beauty of the countryside.

Cover photo: Ha Gorge and its chapel
Title page: on the Lasithi Plateau

Photog... (bottom),
103, ... 29, 29, 30,
31, 4... 117, 122,
129, ... , 62-3, 64,
65, 6... (top), 107
(top ... 40-1, 142,
143, ... wards; 90,
92 (t... 11, 134-5,
136, ...

Line dr...
Maps: ...
contri... StreetMap
comm... (opendata
A CIP ... brary.
Printed ...

☀ Contents

Preface

Mere mention of Crete conjures up all sorts of shimmering images, and we hope that our book — covering the eastern end of the island — will give you the key to some of Crete's mystery and majesty.

The landscapes will hold you spellbound. The surrounding sea — all its vivid shades of blue sparkling in the sun — is part of the scenery too; impossible to separate from the landscape, it's always just in sight, or round the next corner, or disappearing into the skyline.

Woven into the countryside, the people of Crete are yet another part of the landscape. Just a short distance away from all the hubbub and commercialism that a coastline so often creates, a timeless way of life still goes on. Pastoral labours, such as threshing and winnowing, are still carried on without the help of machines. Water is still drawn up from wells.

Whether you walk or drive in Eastern Crete, the mountains will be your constant companions, changing colour and mood from dawn to dusk, as you move through them, round them and over them. You cannot fail to feel their dramatic attraction.

The stunning colours and heady scent of flowers and herbs, tucked into rough ground or splashed across a hillside, the warm-sounding buzz of hovering bees, and the massed band of a thousand cicadas will all leave a lasting impression — the 'special effects' of the total scene.

You may share this rural bliss only with a solitary shepherd, his flocks and dogs, as you walk the hillsides of Eastern Crete. Greeks, on the whole, don't walk, unless they have to for their day's labour, so be prepared for incredulous looks from the townspeople and faint smiles from the villagers — although over the years they have become more accustomed to seeing walkers and, knowingly, will point the way from their *cafeneion* seats or smallholdings!

When we wrote the first edition of this book there were no large-scale maps available, so we had some fun just *finding* our walks, let alone convincing Cretans that we really *wanted* to walk and that other like-minded people were going to come and glory in their countryside as a result of our endeavours.

For Elizabeth and me, compiling the first four editions of this book together over the years was a fitting combination and one that will, we are sure, be of benefit to you. Originally it was Elizabeth's first acquaintanceship with Crete and she was able

5

Elizabeth (left) and Jonnie — on the ground in Crete when writing the first editions of Eastern and Western Crete

to look at it with an inquiring freshness. I, on the other hand, had left a bit of my soul and a lot of my heart there, having lived and worked on the island in the past, so my experience and knowledge was rife with bias! Within days, Elizabeth was immersed in and enchanted by the 'landscape' — and by that I mean the complete 'feeling' of Crete — as well. We're sure you'll share our delight exploring the east and will follow us from here to the *Landscapes of Western Crete*, if you haven't already joined us there.

— JONNIE GODFREY

Recommended reading

John Bowman: *The Travellers' Guide: Crete*
Pat Cameron: *Blue Guide Crete*
Adam Hopkins: *Crete: Past, Present & Peoples*
Nikos Kazantzakis: *Zorba the Greek*
Patrick Leigh Fermor: *Abducting a General*
W Stanley Moss: *Ill Met by Moonlight*
Oleg Polunin: *The Concise Flowers of Europe*
Oliver Rackham and Jennifer Moody: *The Making of the Cretan Landscape*

Agios Therapon, Church of the Life-Giving Spring, on the road to Thripti

Getting about

Hiring a car (or, perhaps better, a 4WD vehicle for the mountain tracks) is certainly the best way to get to know the richness of Eastern Crete. We hope that by giving you some good itineraries, you will be able to make the most of the island — and your car. Many of the tours we suggest take you past the starting- and/or end-points of walks. In fact, seeing the countryside from a car or jeep will encourage you, we hope, to go off the beaten track and into the hills with us, preferably on foot.

Taxis are an alternative way to tour and, particularly if shared, can be a reasonably-priced way to travel. Do agree a fare before you set out, if it's going to be an unmetered journey. Your holiday company's agent or representative will help you to find a driver who will be happy and proud to show off his island.

Organised excursions of one kind or another are always on offer. There are *coach tours*, where you sit back and watch it all go by, *jeep safaris* which take you into the mountains, and *mountain biking* with guided groups.

One of the most entertaining ways of getting about is by **local bus**. Once you've done it for the first time, you'll realise it's economical, reliable and entertaining. You'll whizz along the highways and bumble through villages with a bus-eye view over the countryside. Use the local bus network to explore Eastern Crete economically.

The plans overleaf locate the bus stations in Agios Nikolaos and Iraklion. Timetables for buses covering the eastern half of the island are on pages 157-158. *Note: Even if you have downloaded timetables from the web (see page 157), do pick up a current bus timetable* at the station before you plan any excursions: service frequency changes with the seasons. For complete assurance, verify times in advance by asking. Arrive in good time: buses leave promptly and sometimes even *earlier* than scheduled, particularly those that depart at the crack of dawn. If a bus is full at the depot another one is often laid on. It's better to buy your ticket in the depot before travelling. If you buy tickets on the bus, don't be confused if you get as many as three per person for just one trip; they add up to the total.

In principle, you can flag down buses en route, but they don't *always* stop. *Do* always put your hand out, even at a bus stop!

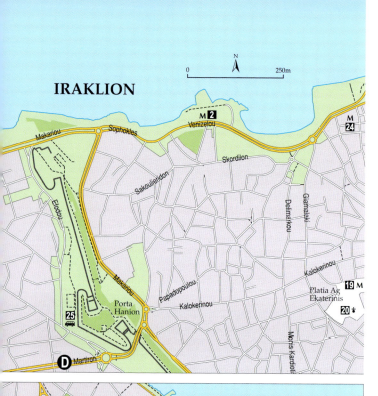

IRAKLION

0   250m

Makaríou

Sophokles

M 2 Venizélou

M 24

Skordilon

Sakoulierídon

Delimatkou

Gjamalaki

Elodou

Makaríou

Kalokerinou

Papadopoulou

Kalokerinou

Platia Ag
Ekaterinis

19 M

20

Porta
Hanion

25

Monís Kardiotí

D Martiron

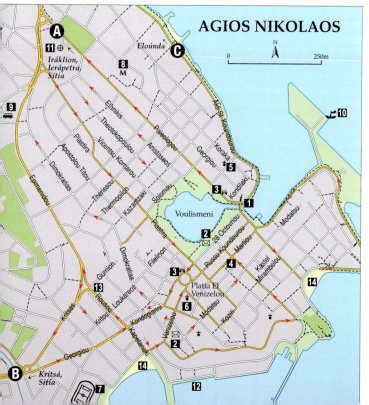

AGIOS NIKOLAOS

0   250m

A

11 ⊕

Iráklion,
Ierápetra,
Sitía

Eloúnda

C

8
M

9

Ethnikís

Theotokopoúlou

Vicentsú Kornárou

Plastira

Apostólou Titou

Dimokratías

Epimenídou

Therissoú

Thermopílon

Kazantzáki

Plastíra

Solomoú

Paleologou

Anastáseos

Georgíou

Koraka

Konialáki

10

5

3

i 1

Voulismeni

2
28 Octovríou

Rusu Koundoúrou

Modatsu

Gurnion

Dimokratías

Filelínon

Kritou

Kondoyiánni

Kapetanáki

Venizélou

Modatsu

Kozeri

Marfou

Kástel
Mirambélou

4

14

Roússu Loukáreos

13

Kitsas

Georgíou

Kritsá,
Sitía

B

7

12

3

6

2

Platía El
Venizélou

14

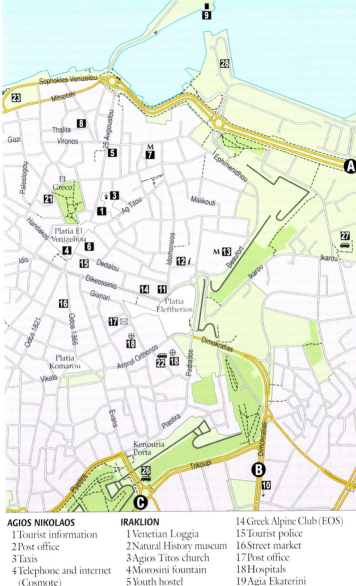

Picnicking and a country code

All the walks in the book offer superb picnic settings, and we mention some of our favourites in the walk headings and highlight them on the walking maps with the symbol *P*, printed in green.

But on days when you are planning only to tour by car, it is helpful to have some idea of where you might stop for an alfresco lunch. Picnicking on Crete is not an organised affair. There aren't any specially-provided sites with tables; it's very much a case of pick your own olive tree and toss for the best views.

Nevertheless, at the top of each car tour we suggest some good places to throw down a towel or a rug (it's unlikely to be wet, but it might well be prickly) and revel in the countryside. Several of our picnic suggestions for the car tours involve a bit of a walk and make good leg-stretchers, but none demand too much climbing or lugging of provisions.

Quite a few of the picnic settings are illustrated — to inspire you!

All picnickers should read the country code below and go quietly in the countryside.

A COUNTRY CODE FOR MOTORISTS AND WALKERS

Observance of certain unwritten rules is essential anywhere in the countryside, but especially on Crete's rugged terrain, where irresponsible behaviour can lead you to cause damage, harm animals, or even endanger your own life.

— **Do not light fires**; everything gets tinder dry.
— **Do not frighten animals.** The goats and sheep you may encounter are not used to strangers. By making a noise, trying to touch or photograph them, you may cause them to run in fear and be hurt.
— **Walk quietly** through all farms, hamlets and villages, and leave all gates just as you found them, wherever they are. Although animals may not be in evidence, the gates *do* have a purpose.
— **Protect all wild and cultivated plants.** Don't pick fruit if it looks like it is somebody else's livelihood. You'll doubtless be offered some en route, anyhow. Avoid walking over cultivated land.
— **Take all your litter** back with you and dispose of it somewhere suitable.
— When **driving**, never block roads or tracks. Park where you will not inconvenience anyone or cause danger.

And especially for walkers:
— **Do not take risks.** Do not attempt walks beyond your capacity and do not wander off the paths described if there is any sign of enveloping cloud or if it is late in the day.
— **Do not walk alone** and *always* tell a responsible person *exactly* where you are going and what time you plan to return. On any but a very short walk near villages, take a mobile, GPS or compass, whistle, torch, extra water and warm clothing, as well as some high energy food, like chocolate. This may sound 'over the top' to an inexperienced walker, but it could save your life.

Harvesting the olives

☀ *Touring*

Crete is a very large island, and most visitors hire a car for some part of their stay to try to get to grips with it.

It pays to hire for a minimum of three days and, while you may find cheaper rates with smaller firms, remember that the larger companies offer the advantage of representation all over the island. Since it's likely that you'll want to cover a lot of ground, you'll be in a better position with a well-known company should anything go wrong.

For general touring covering the whole island, Sunflower recommends the **Michelin** map (1:140,000). To get off the beaten track, we have been using the 1:100,000 maps 'Central Crete' and 'Western Crete' published by **Terrain Cartography**, but *beware:* their 'smooth dirt road' is usually only suitable for 4WD! Remember that your car hire contact will no doubt prohibit off road driving and that **tyres** are *not* covered by insurance; you won't be charged for a simple puncture, but ruined tyres will have to be paid for! Be sure you understand the terms of the hire contract you have signed. Keep your hire contract, passport and driving licence with you at all times when out on the road. Take note of the car hire company's telephone numbers (both office hours and *out of hours*), just in case. **Petrol** is widely available, but it is still a good idea to set out with plenty.

Our car touring notes are brief; they include little information readily available in standard guidebooks or the handouts you can obtain free from tourist offices and tourist information kiosks at home or on Crete. Instead, we've concentrated on the 'logistics' of touring: times and distances, road conditions, and giving clear directions where you might falter or be misled — for instance, by lack of signposting. Most of all, we emphasise possibilities for **walking** and **picnicking**. While some of the suggestions for short walks and picnics may not be suitable during a long car tour, you may find a landscape that you would like to explore at leisure another day. (Note that references in brackets at the top of a tour refer to walks and picnics that can be easily reached by *detouring* off the main route.)

Our pull-out touring maps are ideal for planning and in fact contain all the information you will need outside the towns. The tours have been written up with Agios Nikolaos as departure/return point, but can quite easily be joined from other centres. Plans of Agios Nikolaos and Iraklion are on pages 8-9.

SOME POINTS WORTH NOTING

We cannot stress too strongly the advantage of carrying a good guide to Crete's history and archaeological heritage; see page 6. Note also:

— **Allow plenty of time for visits**; our times for the tours include only very brief stops at viewpoints labelled (☞) in the notes.
— **Telephones** (should you need one) are located at most kiosks, at OTE (telephone exchanges) and in *cafeneions.* Many telephone boxes are card phones; buy cards at kiosks. Calls are metered.
— WC indicates **public toilets**; these are rare, but others are found in restaurants.
— Don't be flummoxed by **Greek road signs**; they are almost invariably followed by English ones.
— You are meant to cross a **solid white line near the edge of the road**, when someone wants to overtake. But beware of slower vehicles, laden donkeys, bikes, etc ahead, when you round bends.
— Conversely, **a solid white line in the middle of the road** means NO OVERTAKING — despite the behaviour of motorists who appear not to notice it.
— **Storms** in 2019/20 left roads in a parlous state: popular tourist routes (Lasithi) were repaired at time of writing; others (Thripti) were still **eroded with potholes**.
— **Do think** before you pull up to admire a view, if you are not at a viewpoint with parking; remember that other motorists cannot see round corners.
— Never throw **cigarette ends** out of the car.
— Come to a standstill at **stop signs**.
— The spelling of **village names** may vary. We have used the letter 'H' where an 'X' or 'CH' might be used locally; this is to aid pronunciation.
— In towns, only **park** your car where permitted.
— In villages it may be difficult to locate the **through road** which may be narrow and unsigned.
— **Priority signs** (red/black/white arrows) on narrow roads give priority to the *black* arrow.

— You will see many **shrines** beside the road (they vary from little boxes topped by a cross and filled with oil, a candle, icon or pictures to very elaborate miniature churches like the one shown above). They warn travellers that sometime in the past a fatal or near-fatal accident involving motor vehicles has occurred at that spot. **Drive carefully!**

Distances quoted are *cumulative kilometres* from Agios Nikolaos. A key to the symbols in the notes is on the touring map. Do note, however, that only the largest churches — or churches that are landmarks — have been highlighted, since every village has at least one church. The same can be said of tavernas or *cafeneions;* food and drink can be found almost anywhere.

All motorists should read the Country code on page 11 and go quietly in the countryside. *Kalo taxithee!*

Car tour 1: THE NORTH AND SOUTH COASTS

Agios Nikolaos • Gournia • Pahia Ammos • Sitia • Piskokefalo • Lithines • Ierapetra • Episkopi • Agios Nikolaos

162km/100mi; 4 hours' driving; very straightforward — all roads are in good condition.
Walks en route: (1-3), 4, 9-13,

(14), 15, 15, (19-20)
Picnic suggestions: Gournia, Kavousi, Exo Mouliana, Makrigialos, (Vasiliki), Monastiraki

---

This 'grand tour' will highlight for you the contrasting landscapes of the north and south coasts. Although the drive from start to finish takes over four hours, it's an excellent day's outing, with good opportunities for swimming and relaxing in varied scenery, or for short walks to fine viewpoints.

We choose to take the '*OLD ROAD*' (🎥) from Agios Nikolaos towards Sitia, but you may prefer the new A90 (🎥). Either way, you quickly pass the turn-off to Kritsa and Mardati (Walks 1-3). The old road then skirts **Almiros** and **Almoudara**, the two beaches (often crowded in high season) just outside Agios Nikolaos that keep the occupants of the many surrounding villas and apartments happy, with their cool, spring-filled bays.

Immediately after the old road joins the A90 (11km), a lane goes under the highway to the sapphire-to-turquoise sea at **Kalo Horio**, shown on page 66; Walk 4 can end there. And almost at once after this is the turning right to the old village of Kalo Horio (🎥) and Prina; Car tour 3 turns off here.

A kilometre further on you may not even notice the Istron Bay Hotel, so attractively has it been concealed. In under 30 minutes you pass the Minoan site of **Gournia**★ (19km 🚻WC), where the remains of an entire village straddle the hillside to the right. The site itself is a pleasant picnic setting; or walk back

along the main road towards Agios Nikolaos, then follow the first track to the left for 15 minutes (turning right at a Y-forks, towards the church). Soon the road hairpins down into the rather drab village of **Pahia Ammos** (21km 🏖🎥M), where there are some surprisingly good fish tavernas by the sea. It is all set against a superb backdrop — the awe-inspiring Thripti Mountains.

Pass the main turning for

Oleanders line the coastal highway on the foothills of the Orno range near Sfaka. Walk 11 takes you up into these hills, which are not as barren as they appear (see photos on pages 54 and 88).

Ierapetra off to the right (22km) and go straight on towards Sitia. This is a particularly attractive coastal route (🚏); the road hugs the hillsides to the right and is never far above the sea to the left. Flowers line the roadside in spring, and the colours and patterns on the hillsides change constantly, as sheer rock and vegetation vie for dominance. Numerous villages are passed, perched on hillsides overlooking the sea.

Pretty **Kavousi** (28km ✝) is the next village of note, nestling in the hills ahead. Walk 12 starts here and takes you up over those glorious hills, to Thripti. There's good picnicking 15-30 above Kavousi if you follow Walk 12, or you could drive to the start of Walk 15c proper, for the views shown on page 99: take the road signposted to 'AZORIA/ VRODA' 250m past the church. Kavousi is the base for an extremely

popular gorge walk which follows an open watercourse for part of the way (Walks 15a-c; photo on page 100).

Not far beyond Kavousi, at **Platanos** (30km ✂), the Panorama Taverna is worth a refreshment stop, as the views over the island of Psira are particularly fine. The road passes a turn-off left down to Mohlos on the coast before running to the right of Lastros (34km). Another road runs down to Mohlos (where you would see the white scar of gypsum quarries) from the next village en route, **Sfaka**. Walk 11 begins here in Sfaka and ends at **Tourloti**. The two villages seem no distance apart at all by road, but the walk makes a pleasant loop through the lovely countryside and farmlands shown on page 88. High above Sfaka, surrounded by wheat fields, you would look out to the Orno range.

At 44km bypass Mirsini (✝), where there is a church with

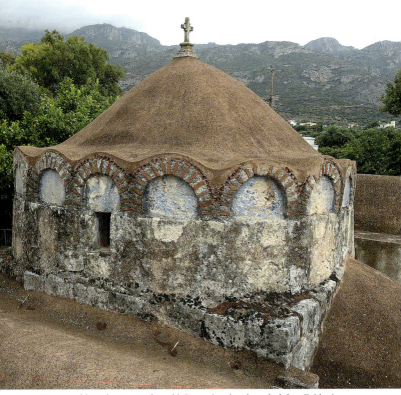

Homeward bound, you pass above this Byzantine church on the left at Episkopi …

attractive Venetian doorways. Note the fine setting of the church above you on the right, too: both the parishioners and the priest can enjoy some wonderful views! From here we descend into **Mesa Mouliana** (53km 🍷), and then the coastal strip widens out and the mountains dwindle to mere hills around **Exo Mouliana** (56km), from where Walk 16 delves into the Richtis Gorge; just below the bridge shown on page 104 there are some lovely picnic places in the gorge.

When you see a hill with ruined stone windmills on it, you'll know you're approaching the Sitia Plain. Keep to the A90 where a road leads down through **Hamezi** (57km **M**), where there's a museum containing local antiquities, and past Skopi (🍷), down to the right. As you near Sitia the landscape is greener and more fertile; olive trees and vines abound. Sitia is known for its sultanas, by the way. After about an hour-and-a-half's driving, ignore the fork left to the port and airport; head right and you'll get your first good look at **Sitia★**, a large, white, sprawling harbour town (68km 🚻♿🏨✕🍷M WC). It's a pleasant place to wander round.

From the roundabout on the main road through Sitia, go right for 'IERAPETRA'; then keep straight ahead

... and the astounding Ha Gorge on the right above Monastiraki just afterwards.

where Vai, Palekastro and Zakros are signposted to the left. Beyond **Piskokefalo** (71km 🏠), the road (follow signs for '*IERAPETRA*') winds through olive groves and low vineyards, and the hills in between are thickly carpeted with shrubs and bushes. The road heads gradually uphill, giving good panoramic views. Before long you pass through **Maronia** (77km), a village tucked almost out of sight below the road stretching out before you. Look out for fresh spring water gushing from the fountain by the side of the road.

Go through **Epano Episkopi**; the road rises again, gradually, into rolling hills flanked by pine,

eucalyptus and plane trees. At 85km, just before **Papagiannides**, there is a taverna with a fresh water source. Then the road dips down into the sizeable village of **Lithines**. About six kilometres past here, you'll see the Kapsa Monastery off to the left on the coast, before coming to the first seaside village on the south coast, **Pilalimata** (98km). Doubtless you'll drive straight through it, eager to see if the rest of the south coast has anything more inspiring to offer.

It has, so press on! At the end of the village, follow signposting left for '*ANALYPSI*' (🏠), leaving the wide bypass road signed to Ierapetra. Drop down into **Analipsi** and you'll come to **Makrigialos** (🚌), from where Walk 20 begins with a taxi ride. What about a swim? There's a pleasant, sandy beach here, with a host of inviting tavernas strung out along it, inviting you to relax ... or you could picnic in the shade of nearby trees or at the churchyard shown on page 115.

After your break, continue past **Koutsouras** (100km; 🚌 at 101km, 102km). Here you are at the edge of what is a large area of market gardening. While all the plastic greenhouses (*thermokipos;* literally 'hot gardens') don't enhance the scenery, they have done wonders for the livelihood of the local people. Forced crops of tomatoes, cucumbers, bananas, melons, courgettes, etc have brought considerable wealth to this area in the last couple of decades.

As you leave Koutsouras, the flat road curves along beside the sea, passing pretty **Galini** (111km 🚌) and **Agia Fotia**, where Walk 10 ends. Both villages are quiet, pleasant places to stop for a swim, before continuing on through **Ferma** (114km 🏨 ✕ 🚌).

On coming into **Ierapetra** (123km 🛈 🏨 ✕ 🚌 ⊕ WC), take note of a dual carriageway signposted right for Agios Nikolaos at traffic lights. One needs to spend some time here: it's a low-key place, full of good fish tavernas and ice-cream and drinks bars. The town beach is pleasant, with the remains of a grand Venetian castle at one end. The library holds a small collection of Minoan *sarcophagi*. Ierapetra is the commercial centre for the plastic greenhouse trade — all fed by the Bramiana Reservoir (Walk 19).

After your visit, return to the dual carriageway and head left (🚌). This road (🚌) whisks you across the island at its narrowest point, via a low-lying isthmus. Less than 14 kilometres of good road separate the Libyan and Cretan seas from south to north. You pass to the left of **Kato Horio**: if you plan to climb Stavromenos one day (Walk 14; photo on pages 96-97), the turn-off is in this village, from where you can drive up to Thripti.

Soon (133km) you come to the bypass for **Episkopi**: it's worth making a foray into this village, to visit the tiny Byzantine church shown on page 16 (⛪). It's a jewel, but easy to miss. You'll find it down to the right of the road, some 50m south of the main village church (which is on the left-hand side of the road). Walk 10 begins here, and Walk 9 ends here.

As you drive through this area, you'll understand why it's such good walking country: just look at those glorious mountains! Pass the turning off left to **Vasiliki**, known for the fine specimens of long-spouted, oddly-coloured ancient pottery found here. Vasiliki is the starting point for Walk 9, which takes you into the foothills of the Dikti Mountains, shown on pages 79 and 80. There's fine picnicking about 20 minutes along the walk. Opposite the Vasiliki turn-off, slicing through the Thripti range, is the striking **Ha Gorge**, above **Monastiraki** (reached via the next turning to the right). It's hard to imagine from this vantage point, but Walk 12 brings you down to this road from above and behind the gorge, shown on the previous page — whereas Walk 13 takes you right into its jaws — a great place to picnic, shown on page 95!

From here you'll soon approach the north coast (🚌 at 140km). Turn left and make for **Agios Nikolaos** on your outbound route (162km).

Car tour 2: THE FAR EAST AND KATO ZAKROS

Agios Nikolaos • Sitia • Toplou Monastery • Vai • Palekastro • Kato Zakros • Sitia • Agios Nikolaos

241km/150mi; 6h30min-7h driving. This is a marathon, but you will be glad you've done it! As it's a long way, the driving is best shared. Kato Zakros is a nice place to overnight.

Walks en route: Walks (1-3), 11, 12, 15, 16, (30)
Picnic suggestions: Gournia, Kavousi, Exo Mouliana, (Rousolakos or Hiona Beach), Zakros Source

This excursion takes you to a monastery, a famous Minoan site, beaches in contrasting settings and wild countryside. It includes a detour to a less well-known Minoan site and beach — a wonderfully exhilarating, if somewhat tiring, day's outing.

Set off by using the notes on page 14 (Car tour 1) for the first 68km of this tour. You won't have much time for stops; it will take you well over an hour and a half to reach **Sitia★** (68km ⛽🚻♿🏛️✕🅿️MWC). Keep to Car tour 1 past the roundabout, but at the traffic lights where that tour goes straight on for Ierapetra, turn left for 'VAI/PALEKASTRO/ZAKROS'. The road turns left down to the coast, then right, to continue past Sitia's beach. You then cross a narrow bridge and drive past Agia Fotia (71km 🅿️) into low-lying, rugged brown hills and some rather uninteresting countryside — until the large Dionysis holiday complex springs into view (78km). Built in the style of an authentic Greek village, it ran into difficulties well before the pandemic; it's now a ghost town, permanently closed. Thereafter the landscape becomes greener and more interesting with some wonderful large rocks and boulders around. If you're lucky, the heady aroma of wild thyme will be all around you.

Now the road twists uphill, following the coastline. At 80km turn left for Toplou. The road climbs up again through barren landscape; you may well have to stop for a herd of goats, hundreds of which belong to the monastery up ahead, **Toplou★** (84km ♿). The small 17th-century church has a lovely bell tower. Inside are some particularly interesting icons. Beyond its architectural beauty, what impresses one most about Toplou is its splendid isolation … except for a wind farm east of the monastery which can be seen from miles away.

Continue on the same road past the monastery; ten minutes along will bring you in sight of the palm trees at Vai. Keep straight on where Palekastro and Zakros are signposted to the right; after 3km you come into **Vai★** (94km ✕). If it's summer, you may not be able to see the palm tree-fringed sandy beach for people! If you don't mind crowds, this is a good place to have a swim, although sunbeds are expensive and you have to pay to park. But Vai is much prettier out of season.

After a quick break, press on. You're bound for one of Crete's gems, and it's important to leave enough time for your visit. Leave Vai's beach and, after 1.2km, turn left. Then take the next left for Palekastro, 10 minutes away. The road passes through cultivated countryside, planted with olive trees and vines.

At **Palekastro** (106km ♿✕🅿️), on reaching the square, turn sharp left in front of the church, then turn right for 'ZAKRO' some 80m further on (or keep more or less straight on for Walk 30). The road climbs for a while, then continues along a fertile valley. Olive groves abound; imagine how many there must be on the island. This road weaves its way through interesting small villages set in attractive heathland. First pass through **Lagada,** then **Hohlakies** — which is *really* small — and then climb out of the valley. Come into **Azokeramos**, go on through pretty, open countryside, and then head down again, to **Kelaria,** another tiny hamlet, with a stone-walled fountain on the right. As you head towards the next village, **Adravasti**, perched on the hillside, the soil changes to a striking wine colour.

You pass another fresh-water fountain about 50 metres short of the sign for the village of Zakros. Here's a chance to picnic in the lovely setting shown on page 107: turn right, uphill, 80m past the fountain. Continue uphill round several bends, to the end of the road. There is a small white chapel here with beautiful carvings, and a deep ravine with a path alongside it, leading after 200m to a plane tree with seating and running water even after a dry summer. This is the **Zakros Source**, visited during Walk 17. Apart from the Natural History

A priest at Toplou catches up on the news; opposite: palm beach at Vai

and Water Mill museums (daily ex Mondays from 11.00-18.00), there is nothing of special interest in **Zakros** (124km 🛏️ ✕ 🚏), so drive on, turning right in the 'square' for Kato Zakros, which really *is* worth the time and distance. Ignore the sign for Xerokambos to the right; keep straight ahead.

Five kilometres past Zakros (you will have passed the starting point for Alternative walk 18-1), the road hurtles down the side of a hill, with a ravine on the right and only the sea in sight ahead. Drive carefully for the next 4km, until you come into delightful **Kato Zakros★** (129km 🛏️; photo on page 109), with its beautiful bay, beach and peaceful seclusion, only marred by lunchtime coaches. The Minoan Palace of Zakro is behind the beach. Excavation started here at the beginning of the century, and more work has taken place since 1962, revealing the ruins of a late Minoan palace, all on one level — and easier to 'reconstruct' in the mind's eye than some of the other sites on the island. Behind the palace, in the gorge (Walk 18), there are caves that

were used for Minoan burials — some as high as 200m/650ft above the valley floor. Before you explore the site, however, you may well head for the beach, since by this time you're likely to be both tired from driving and famished. Around the bay are several pleasant tavernas with open barbecues for grilled delights; it's particularly pleasant in the evening to sit by the sea and watch supper being cooked.

When time runs out, retrace your route up the steep mountainside, back to **Zakros** and on to **Palekastro** (155km). Here turn hard left into the main square (signed 'SITIA') and then keep straight on (🚏) towards Sitia, passing the turning for Toplou Monastery off to the right. At **Sitia**, turn left at the end of the town beach, following 'AGIOS NIKOLAOS'. At the traffic lights go right (same signposting). Then take the second exit from the roundabout, to reverse your route from earlier in the day. You'll climb up out of Sitia and follow the good coastal road all the way back to **Agios Nikolaos** — about an hour and a half's driving from here (241km).

Agios Nikolaos • Kalo Horio • Kalamafka • Anatoli • Gra Ligia •
Ierapetra • Episkopi • Agios Nikolaos

See also photos on pages 16, 66, 92, 94, 95 and 111	Walks en route: Walks 4, 5, 9, 10, 12, 13, (14, 19)
85km/53mi; 2h30min driving. Half of this trip is on winding country roads.	Picnic suggestions: Kalamafka, (Bramiana Reservoir, Vasiliki), Monastiraki

It doesn't take long to reach the south coast from Agios Nikolaos if you just go straight there and back via the main road, skirting the western edge of the Thripti mountains. But it makes a pleasant change to drive one way through the gentler hills and pretty villages to the west.

Leave Agios Nikolaos by using the notes on page 14, heading towards Sitia. Tourism has spread from the hub of Agios (thankfully it hasn't stacked upwards as well), out as far as the main road below Kalo Horio. At 11km (some 15 minutes' driving), turn right for 'MESELERI/ KALO CHORIO/KALAMAFKA' and 'PRINA'. Soon you'll notice the change: you're in the Cretan countryside!

The road winds up through the old village of **Kalo Horio** (12km ✕). (Walk 4 would take you from the enchanting village of Kroustas down through this village and to the coast shown on page 66.) From here we carry on over pine-covered hills, with a steep drop to one side. Notice the pale colouring of the limestone-based soil.

At a Y-fork a little over 5km from Kalo Horio go right for 'PRINA', leaving the road to Meseleri off to the left. We skirt to the left of **Prina** (18km), perched on a hillside, and keep climbing upwards through olive groves and hills cloaked in clover. About 5km south of Prina there is a wonderful viewpoint to the left of the road (🖼); you can look out over the south coast to the Libyan Sea beyond the large reservoir south of Agios Georgios on the Lasithi Plateau.

Kalamafka (25km ✝), where Walk 5 starts, is tucked into a hollow and dominated by the church on Kastelos Hill. You could picnic in the setting shown opposite at the Kefalavrisi spring by either walking or driving the first 15 minutes of Walk 5 (page 68). Otherwise, about 1km past the church, turn right at the T-junction for 'ANATOLI' and 'MALES'. Orange and lemon trees flourish in this sheltered area; but soon we're climbing through pines and scrub again. Massive rock formations create imposing natural sculptures.

Soon come into **Anatoli** (33km). This is such a pretty village that you may want to stretch your legs by wandering through the maze of alleyways down to the left of the road. On the far side of Anatoli, at a triangular 'roundabout' with a statue in the middle, turn left. The road turns down below Anatoli and then snakes quite steeply down the mountainside. Pines give way to olive trees as the coastal plain comes completely into view, straight down across the spread of Ierapetra.

Soon the road evens out and you drive through **Kalogeri**, where there is a stone fountain on the right where you can collect fresh spring water. Continue past a pretty church (✝), also on the right. As you

Kefalavrisi, the gushing source above Kalamafka, is a lovely picnic setting. Walk 5 crosses the stream here before following the track shown on pages 68-69 to Kroustas — the track is part of the well-waymarked E4 route. Kefalavrisi is one of the sources of the Bramiana Reservoir (Walk 19), a bird sanctuary. On the way back to Agios Nikolaos, you could call in at Episkopi and Monastiraki, where there's a pleasant taverna (shown below) on the route of Walks 12 and 13.

approach the coast, bamboo proliferates.

It's rather a disappointment to come down to this part of the south coast, after the beauty of the hills behind us. Unattractive plastic greenhouses, full of tomatoes, courgettes, cucumbers, bananas and melons announce the industry of the region. When the *meltemi* wind blows here — at the height of summer — swathes of plastic rip and run riot across the surrounding countryside, before flying into the sea.

When you come to the main south coast road (46km), turn left into **Gra Ligia** (☎). You *can* get to the Bramiana Reservoir for Walk 19 from here, but you might find it more straightforward to take the Kalamafka road from the large red-domed church just before **Ierapetra** (50km). Use the notes beginning on page 18 to visit the town and then return on the main north/south road, via **Episkopi** and the **Ha Gorge**, to **Agios Nikolaos** (85km).

Car tour 4: A MINOAN ODYSSEY

Agios Nikolaos • Malia • (Iraklion) • Gortys • Agii Deka • Festos • Matala • Agii Deka • Houdetsi • (Knossos) • Agios Nikolaos

300km/186mi; over 6 hours' driving, but all on main roads, so easy throughout. You may wish to keep to the A90, rather than take our suggested *route via Malia and Hersonisos.*
Walks en route: 24 (end)
Picnic suggestions: Festos, Agia Triada, Matala

Setting out on this tour you may feel, as we do, that you're embarking on a pilgrimage of sorts; there's something very intriguing about Crete's Minoan past. The famous sites are a 'must', on everyone's itinerary. Even if you don't wish to spend a great deal of time at any particular site, this excursion is worthwhile: it takes in all the highlights and follows an exceptionally scenic route. While you *could* return to Iraklion by crossing the island on the main north/south road (and perhaps, if you want more time at the sites you will choose to do this), we'd like you to see a bit more of the countryside, so we have mapped out a different route for your homeward journey.

From Agios Nikolaos, take the main road to Iraklion (Exit A; Paleologou Street). Go straight ahead to the A90 highway at the traffic lights on the far side of town. You're swiftly on your way. After about 11km, look up to the left: the highest village you see is Vrises (Walk 21), on the route to Lasithi. No doubt you'll visit this area at some point (it's fine walking country) — perhaps going via Neapolis, which is the next large town you pass, again on the left. The region's courthouse is at Neapolis. The windmills you pass by now, ranged up the hill both below and above the road, were used to grind corn. A sign of the times: they're now still. Beyond Neapolis, just before Vrahasi (set up on a hill to the right), go through a short tunnel (17.5km). Walk 24 ends by this tunnel. Remember to switch off your headlights.

Soon go through **Selinari** (21.5km ♦✕WC); the church of Agios Georgios is up above the road. It's worth looking skywards here — you might be lucky enough to see an eagle soaring over the mountains. As

you pass the church, the view opens out and the sea comes into sight down at Sisi. At 25km take the turn-off right for Malia (its archaeological site is visited in Car tour 7), *leaving* the A90 highway. The road first goes through the spread of **Malia★** (29km ♦▲✕🖃⊕) — some people like it, others keep going. Its famous crowded beach is down a side street, off to the right.

We move on, at **Agios Dimitrios** keeping straight ahead at the traffic lights on the 'IRAKLION OLD NATIONAL ROAD'. Go through **Stalida** and past the mammoth Sofokles pot emporium, then through **Hersonisos** (37km ▲✕🖃 M WC), which has a relatively pleasant waterfront strand on the other side of all the shops and an outdoor Museum of Traditional Cretan Life.

Forge ahead, through **Kato Gouves** (🖃). At 47.5km the old road strikes off right to Iraklion, via the coast; keep straight ahead on the A90 highway ('IRAKLION NEW ROAD'). Dia island is in view by now. Soon you'll pass Iraklion's nearest

Matala: the caves here, once inhabited by hippies, are carved in a high ochre cliff. No one knows who first used them, and they vary in size and 'furnishings'.

good beach, Kokkini Hani. We suggest you bypass Iraklion today. Having passed to the south of the city, on the west side of the built-up area, turn right for Mires (68km; signposted 'MOIRES'). Then turn right again, under the highway bridge (signed for 'TYMPAKI' and 'MOIRES'). Now just keep straight on along the wide 97 road.

When the road (with ample 🚽) narrows to just two lanes, the going could be slower, although this road is being constantly improved to carry the fairly heavy traffic from Iraklion to Festos and Gortys. It bypasses turnings to Siva, Venerato, the Paliani Monastery, Kerasia and Avgeniki — as well as quite a long list of wineries! Looking to the right (at around 84km), there is a most appealing view over verdant rolling vineyards. Eventually the road climbs straight up through the hills to **Agia Varvara** (94km 🚽). Its chapel, set on a rock, comes into view some time before the village. Legend has it (wrongly) that the geometric centre of Crete is close by.

Continuing south, you're on a new road, eventually giving a far-reaching panorama over the **Mesara Plain** — 5km wide and 30km east to west — Crete's largest expanse of *flat*

land and certainly a fertile splash amidst all the brown mountains. Descending now to the plain, a road joins from the right and you go through a tunnel, after which two lanes are devoted to northbound traffic. Beyond a second tunnel, you're on a dual carriageway.

When you come to a T-junction (106.5km) turn left towards 'AGII DEKA'. Once again on a two-lane road, pass the new Archaeological Museum of Mesara (M✗WC) on the right, which opened in 2020 with an exhibition of Minoan seafaring and navigation. Just past it, on the left, is a derelict factory advertising Bell's Scotch Whisky… Then you spot the remains of the basilica of Agios Titos on the left.

Pull into the car park for **Gortys★** (109km 🚻🚹✗WC), a Dorian site of great importance and once the capital of Crete, with a population that may have reached 300,000. Legend has it that Zeus and Europa cavorted here (look for the plane tree where it all happened). Agios Titos stands in front of Gortys: according to the Bible, St Titus was commissioned by St Paul to convert the Cretans.

Leaving Gortys, continue straight on towards 'AGII DEKA'.

Under 1km past Gortys, there's a sign on the right for '*TOMBS AGII DEKA 100M*'. Turn in right here and after just under 200m you will come to the (modern) chapel containing the Tombs of the Ten Cretan Martyrs★ (♟; 'Agii Deka' means 'Holy Ten'). Should you wish also to see the few graphic icons in the 16th-century church in the centre of **Agii Deka**★ (♟), you can walk there from here; it's just 150m.

From here we continue west through **Kapariana** (117km ✗🍴WC). Now referring to the map of Western Crete, continue through **Mires** (118km 🏔✗🍴⊕) and past the monastery of Panagia Kalivianis on the right (123km), now an orphanage and convalescent home. Within striking distance of Festos (🍴), up on the hill, turn left for '*FAISTOS*' (125.5km). There are more good views as you climb above the plain (📷). Then you reach the high point of today's pilgrimage, **Festos**★ (127.5km 🛖✗📷WC). As you walk from the car to the site, breathe deeply and inhale the scent of pines. And then take in the view! The Minoans certainly knew how to choose their settings. It's a glorious viewpoint towards the Dikti and Lasithi mountains to the east, the Ida range to the north and the Asterousia to the south. At the tourist pavilion you'll find all the information you need to help you make the most of your visit.

When you leave, don't miss **Agia Triada**★ (🛖), the remains of a summer palace in a delightful setting. To get to it, carry on through the car park at Festos and fork right. This turning will take you back down towards the Mesara Plain, to a spot from where you can walk down to the site in three minutes. Just imagine it: some say the sea came right up to this palace.

When you've had your fill of Crete's fascinating past, you might entertain thoughts of a swim. Anyway, you must see the famous caves of Matala. So take the road back to Festos and, at the junction before the car park, turn sharp right for Matala. There's a pretty church on the left, surrounded by the customary cypresses. Pass to the right of Agios Ioannis and some 3.5km south of the Festos car park, turn right for '*MATALA*' (🍴). **Pitsidia** (139km ✗) is the next pretty village, but **Matala** (143km ∩🛖🏔✗WC) has a fine sweep of sand, and some

Festos and the Mesara Plain

trees for shade if you picnic there.

When the time comes to head back to Agios Nikolaos, drive off in the direction you came and, at the roundabout (148km) turn left to round **Pitsidia**. (About 1km west of Pitsidia is Komos Beach, a very long, sandy, quiet beach with an important archaeological site by the sea.) Follow the road back to **Festos** (156km) and drive through the car park, back down to the main 97 road. Turn right here for Iraklion (158km).

You head back across the **Mesara Plain**. At the junction on the far side of **Agii Deka**, turn right at the signpost for '*GANGALES/PIRGOS*' (173km). The road travels through olive groves and almond trees. Past the narrow streets of **Gangales** (177km) you glimpse pretty Stoli ahead to the right. The vista across the plain is really magnificent: the greens of the foreground spreading and merging into the browns in the distant mountains. Drive through **Stoli** (182km 🐾) and turn right at the crossroads just over 1km outside the village ('*ASIMI/PYRGOS*'). Head on through **Asimi** (186km 🐾). Two kilometres further on, stay on the main road, which curves round to the right past a solar farm on the left; then head straight on, following '*VIANNOS*' (beside an isolated church on the right). At the large round-about 4km further on (194km), take the third exit for '*IRAKLIO*'.

Ligortinos (198km 🐾) is up to your right. The landscape around here looks like an embroidery sampler, with all its different stitches, green and brown. The route is straightforward now, skirting **Tefeli** (199km 🐾🐾), **Armanogia** and the dot on the landscape called **Partheni** (211km). At the major fork 3.5km past Partheni, keep right for '*IRAKLIO*'. Soon you reach **Houdetsi** (215km 🐾🐾), **Agios Vasilios**

(217km 🐾) and **Kaloni** (219km). At the far end of Kaloni you have a choice. *You can take the bypass,* saving only about 7km in distance but half an hour or more in time: turn left on the main road for '*IRAKLIO*', then turn right at once ('*IRAKLIO*'). Once in Iraklion, when you can see the elevated A90 highway crossing your road up ahead, *get into the left-hand lane before the traffic lights* — there is no filter right to access the eastbound highway.

Otherwise keep to the old road: at the junction outside Kaloni turn left, then keep straight on for '*PEZA*'. Very soon you'll see the north coast again, over the brow of a hill. First go through **Peza** (221km 🐾🐾) and **Kounavi** (223km 🐾🐾). Approaching Patsides (227km) you again have the choice: to stay on the old road go left for Arhanes, then right for '*IRAKLIO/PATSIDES*'. Go through **Patsides** and **Ampela** (🐾). Ignore the fork right for Skalani outside Ampela; go straight on for '*KNOSSOS*'. Beyond **Spilia** (231km 🐾) you pass just to the right of an attractive aqueduct at **Agia Irini**, built during the brief occupation of Crete by the Egyptians in the middle of the 19th century. Further on, keep a look-out for a brief view of Knossos, hidden away in the cypress trees over to your right.

We suggest that you save your visit to Knossos and the museum at Iraklion for another day (Car tour 10). Certainly your visit to the museum will be more meaningful now that you've seen some of the sites that yielded its treasures. Leaving Knossos on your right (🐾), drive into **Iraklion**. Go straight on until you see the elevated A90 high-way crossing your road up ahead. Keep in the right-hand lane to turn onto the highway here, and head back to **Agios Nikolaos** (300km).

Car tour 5: THE AGIOS IOANNIS PENINSULA

**Agios Nikolaos • Elounda • Plaka • Vrouhas • Loumas • Skinias • Karidi
• Pines • Agios Nikolaos**

See also photos on pages 51, 72,
74, 75, 76 and 77
*60km/37mi; 2h15min driving. Late
afternoon sun spreads a wonderful light
over this glorious scenery, but this easy
drive can be made at any time of day.*

*Roads are mostly in good condition. No
petrol for 40km beyond Elounda.*
Walks en route: Walks 6, 7b, 8
Picnic suggestions: above Plaka or
the Agios Efrain chapel (see map on
page 74), above Pano Elounda

H ere's one of the prettiest short drives you could hope for:
it takes you onto the Agios Ioannis Peninsula, pointing
out into the Sea of Crete towards the distant isles of Karpathos
and Rhodes.

Leave Agios Nikolaos via Exit C
(Akti Koundourou), driving straight
along the sea front in Agios
Nikolaos, past the Minos Beach and
Mirabello hotels. Before long turn
up and right onto the signposted
Elounda road. At 5.5km out of
Agios Nikolaos there is a splendid
viewpoint (📷) by the S-shaped
'Mirum' building, looking down
over the causeway at Olous, towards
Elounda, and — in the distance —
the island of Spinalonga. The Agios
Ioannis Peninsula stretches beyond
Plaka as far as the eye can see.
Driving downhill (☕ at 7.2km), still
taking in the view, pass turnings off
right to several luxury hotels.

Come into **Elounda★** (9.5km
▲✖⊕), where 'Who Pays the
Ferryman?', a popular TV series of
the 1970s, was filmed (as was 'The
Lotus Eaters' in the '60s). Three
sides of the village square are given
over to tavernas, coffee shops and
bars, while the fourth is open to the
sea and usually busy with boats.
Walks 6 and 8 are based on Elounda.
Driving through the village, turn
right behind the church and clock
tower. The road hems the sparkling
sea all the way along to **Plaka** (13km
🛉✖). Plaka has won fame more
recently than Elounda, thanks to
Victoria Hislop's best-selling novel
about nearby Spinalonga, *The Island,*

which greatly increased tourism.
Plaka is one of our favourite swimming spots, even though after
enjoying the clear silky-soft water,
you have to make yourself
comfortable on large rounded stones
to sunbathe.

Tear yourself away from Plaka:
drive along behind the beach and
start climbing up the long steep hill
that cuts across the mountain. Some
4km out of the village, take a right-
hand at a small black and white sign
indicating 'ΑΓ ΙΟΑΝΝΗΣ' — just
before a church and some sail-less
corn mills up ahead on the right
(18km) and you will come to a
perfect picnic spot high over
Spinalonga and Kolokithia. A bit
further along is Agios Efraim chapel,
another good picnic spot. You could
park there for easy Walk 7b — or at
the corn mills.

Then return to the main road and
continue up to **Vrouhas** (19km). A
stone-built fountain in the village is
good for quenching thirst. Go
through the village and continue
towards Loumas. Pass a sign for
Selles, a village set down off to the
right, and drive on up through a
landscape almost 'cluttered' with
stone walls. Only a few scatterings of
shrubs and olive trees are to be seen.

After **Kato Loumas** (22km 🛉)
carry on to **Pano Loumas**, past

28

The crystal-clear sea at Plaka

more corn mills, through olive groves, and always with the sea in sight. In **Skinias** (26km), turn left at the fork, leaving Vlichadia and Agios Georgios off to the right, then blink past the handful of houses and church at **Valtos**. The views are beautiful. At 28km the road forks; take the left hand fork, signposted to Karidi. (The right fork goes cross country to Neapolis.) The road makes sharp bends, ravens circle above and, beyond the olive-clad hills, the scenery becomes more barren and shrub-covered. Soon you'll pass the **Aretios Monastery**, just to the left of the road and, after another bend or two, look down on the red roofs and church of **Karidi** (it means 'walnut'; 37km). It's

worth stopping at this village. Set into the hills are stone houses, once luxury accommodation for goats and sheep. This area is a miniature, very fertile plain, with huge stone wells, corn mills — and a friendly *cafeneion*. Back on the road, 1km further on drive through **Dories**, where you'll pass the village reservoir on your left. Keep left through Dories; in a few minutes there's another marvellous view — looking east to the mountains round Kavousi and Thripti, settings for Walks 12-15.

Now descend past olive groves and vines and, at a fork, turn left for Elounda. Soon reach a splendid viewpoint (📷) over Pines and Elounda. Below **Pines** (43km) the road crosses the path of Walk 8 at the charming house shown on page 77. Then, if you can park safely, the map on page 76 shows a shaded picnic setting by a small church above **Pano Elounda**. Take a break back in **Elounda** itself (47km) and then it's back to **Agios Nikolaos** (60km).

Elounda's clock tower and harbour

Car tour 6: FROM HILL VILLAGE TO SHEPHERD COMMUNITY

Agios Nikolaos • Kritsa • Katharon Plateau • Agios Nikolaos

See also photos on pages 40-41, 53, 58 and 64
50km/31mi; under 2 hours' driving.

The road from Agios Nikolaos to Kritsa is good and wide. From Kritsa to Katharon all the way is asphalted but not always built up at the side, and will be unnerving for some drivers and passengers. No petrol for 34km beyond Kritsa.
Walks en route: Walks 1, 2, 3, 22
Picnic suggestions: Mardati, Lato

This short excursion takes you up from the hubbub of Agios Nikolaos into the heart of the shepherd community in no time. You'll drive steadily upwards until you reach the Katharon Plateau. If you visit in the first days of May, you may be lucky enough to spot the Cretan 'transhumance' — goats and sheep so tightly packed into pickups that they manage to stay upright as their shepherd drivers round the hairpin bends at a speed. On your way back you'll feel you've been a visitor to another world.

In Kritsa's back streets

Leave Agios Nikolaos as for Car tour 1 on page 14 and take the 'KRITSA' turning (1.5km 🅿). You'll pass through **Mardati** (5km) — no more than a scattering of houses. Walk 3 starts here; 15-20 minutes into that walk, there's a lovely picnic setting looking out over Kritsa and the Lasithi Mountains.

Kritsa and the hills beyond come into sight just before **Panagia Kera★** (🛉), the gem of a church shown on pages 40-41; it cherishes some 13th-century frescoes. If there is a string of tourist coaches parked here now, go on and hope to have a look on the way back, when there is a chance that the crowd will only consist of *you*.

Just before the one-way system takes you into the centre of Kritsa, the Dorian site of Lato (shown on page 57) is indicated to the right. This is the starting point for Walk 1 — and there's another lovely picnic spot along that road, with the view to Kritsa shown on page 58. We're sure you'll want to make a stop at **Kritsa★** (8km ✕🅿; Walks 1, 2 and 22), one of our favourite places. It's an attractive hill village, where some of the *cafeneions* have fantastic panoramic views straight out over the Mirabello Gulf. Don't just stay on the main street, however. Wander up or down behind it and have a closer look. People won't mind, if you greet them pleasantly.

A superb viewpoint on the road to Avdeliako

Back in the car, follow the one-way system by taking the right-hand fork uphill through Kritsa. Follow the main street up to the right at an intersection (where the one-way system ends) then, after just 100m, at a Y-fork, turn left for 'KROUSTA/PRINA/PLATEAU OF KATHARO'. The road bends left (signed to Kroustas and Prina), then quickly comes to a three-way junction where you go right for 'PLATEAU OF KATHARO' and curl back to circle Kritsa to the west. Then the road climbs up and into the hillside; it's a long pull, but you'll be rewarded by splendid views over the Mirabello Gulf and Kalo Horio. Halfway up, you'll pass a jeep track off right to Tapes. The hillsides are covered with gorse bushes and spiny shrubs which, as you get

higher, tend to look like crouching animals.

Take heart when you're halfway up and wondering if it's going to be worth the effort. The scenery becomes less lunar-like, and soon trees appear, counteracting the stark-ness. At 19km you lose sight of the sea for a while, tall trees cluster along the road, making a pleasant change of mood, and you pass the splendid viewpoint shown below. A few kilometres further on, there is evidence of another 'living planet'. Two kilometres before your goal the **Katharon Plateau** begins and, to prove it, there are patches of cultivated land, a small vineyard or two, beehives, and two chapels. Shortly after this, you come upon **Avdeliako** (also called Katharon; 25km) and the welcome sight of two tavernas and shady walnut trees. There is good picnicking nearby, too — especially if you follow the E4 (either straight ahead past the little church and towards the Lasithi Plateau or to the left towards Males and Selakano). Shepherds, some-times together with their families, live up here from the first days of May until the beginning of winter. And it is a very popular area for families from Kritsa to come for Sunday lunch — at a barbecue or in a taverna. The peace and quiet is heavenly… unless a jeep safari arrives from Lasithi!

If you have a 4WD vehicle (and the map recommended on page 12), it's also worth bumping along the E4 track at the left of the church to the point where you have good views over the Lasithi Plateau — or you could even carry on to Mesa Lasithi; you would emerge at the point where Walk 22 starts.

Returning the same way from Avdeliako, you'll be back in **Agios Nikolaos** after 50km.

Car tour 7: THE LASITHI PLATEAU

Agios Nikolaos • Neapolis • Mesa Potami • Psychro • Krasi • Mohos • Malia • Agios Nikolaos

See also photos on pages 1, 120-121, 126-127, 138 and 142
117km/73mi; about 4 hours' driving. Although the route is straightforward, it's a tiring one. Lots of hairpin bends *demand cautious driving.*
Walks en route: 21-24, (25), 26, 27
Picnic suggestions: Vrises, Lasithi Plateau, Psychro, (Nisimos Plateau, Roza Gorge)

Most people want to see Lasithi. This is a good day's excursion, taking in not only the plateau but some lovely mountain scenery, an archaeological site, and a sandy beach as well.

Again, we choose to take the 'IRAKLIO OLD ROAD' from Agios Nikolaos, but there is no reason why you shouldn't take the A90. The old road takes you into **Limnes** (where Walk 21 begins and ends); further on, follow the 'PLATEAU OF LASITHI' signs into the large square at **Neapolis** (13km ▲✕🍽⊕M), with its imposing church. Turn left at the top of the square, by the Archaeological Museum, and wind up the hillside.

You drive through the lush and fertile valley of Lakonia and up past the **Kremaston Monastery** (⛪) to **Vrises** (16km). The village church makes a good picnic spot from

Below: you've seen the postcards, now try the walk! We call them windmills, but these are really wind pumps, with nearby water tanks (as can be seen in the photograph on pages 126-127). Right: mist falls on the Homo Sapiens Museum at the Ambelos Pass

where the view over Neapolis and to the hills beyond is excellent. It's just one of a few picnic places along the route of Walk 21. Another road comes in from Agios Nikolaos at 20km: turn right here for the 'PLATEAU OF LASITHI'. You'll drive through **Kato Amigdali** (24km) and, as you come into **Amigdali** 1km further on, look ahead to the towering mountainside, and you will see the scree that Walk 22 takes you across. It's not too difficult a walk, just long!

The lucky passengers can now enjoy stunning views over the

countryside to Mirabello Bay and over the surrounding hills and mountains ahead. The less fortunate driver negotiates hair-pin bends! A taverna just ouside **Zenia** (28km ✕) may offer morning coffees. The hillsides around here are dotted with broom and gorse and, at **Exo Potami** (33km), where there is a church and monument dedicated to war victims, you'll find an even greener landscape, with tall cypress trees, almond, walnut, fruit trees and vineyards. ('Potami' means 'river', which would account for the verdant growth.) **Rousakiana** is next, followed by **Mesa Potami** (36km ✕), where excursion coaches and local buses stop en route for the plateau. The bustling **Skapanis** emporium (41km ✕) is a lone outpost between villages.

And soon you'll have your first glimpse of the edge of the **Lasithi Plateau★**. Under 1km past Skapanis a white arrow signpost signals a

There are tavernas galore on Lasithi, but this colourful spot in Rousakiana caught our eyes as they prepared for visitors in early May after the pandemic.

track off left where Walk 22 begins; there's a fine picnic setting about 10 minutes along, with wonderful views of the plateau. Past **Mesa Lasithi**, by a large church on the left (46km ✝), turn left for Psychro. Go through **Agios Konstandinos** and keep straight on, leaving a turning back to the main road to Agios Nikolaos off to the left. **Agios Georgios** (48km ✝🏠M) has a Cretan folklore museum in its midst — well worth a visit.

Now, as the road starts to climb, the plateau comes into full view,

showing off just some of its windmills. Pass through **Avrahontes** (🏠), **Kaminaki** (✗), and the narrow street of **Magoulas**. Soon you're in **Psychro** (53km 🏔✗🏠 and freshwater fountain). If you would like to visit the Diktaion ('Dikti') Cave (or picnic in the shade nearby), take the road curving up left to a parking area and viewpoint (55km ∩🖼). To really appreciate the windmills of Lasithi, leave your car here and walk a while along the route of easy Walk 23.

Continue the tour by returning

to the main road that hems the plateau and turn left (signposted to Kato Metohi). The road goes via **Plati** and **Kato Metohi** (59km), then passes the **Vidianis Monastery** off to the left. Having almost completed a circuit of the plateau, at 64km, just past the Panorama Taverna, turn left for 'IRAKLIO'. (But go straight on here towards Tzermiado if you're planning to try circular Walk 25 or picnic at the Nismos Plateau shown on pages 134-135.) Up on the hill ahead there are some eye-catching old mills standing sentry on the skyline at the Ambelos Pass and marking your departure from the plateau. The road climbs and soon there is a panorama far below you, straight over to the north coast (☞).

Go through **Kera** (66km ✝), a staging post on Walks 26 and 27, and past the turning for **Moni Kardiotissas**; then turn right off the road and into **Krasi** (✕WC). It's worth making this short detour here to see one of the island's plane trees classified as 'monumental'; it's set in the middle of the village. Opposite it there is a freshwater fountain. Such is the attraction of this plane that there are tavernas galore in the village. (Kavousi's monumental plane, visited on Walks 12 and 15, is too far off the beaten track to attract tavernas.)

Driving on through Krasi, carry straight on at a junction, ignoring a road off right to Malia. You are back on the main road, driving down towards the coast. Some 3km along, the main tour turns right for 'MOCHOS'. (But if you have time and would like to picnic in the lovely setting shown on pages 140-141, keep straight on for another 3km, then turn sharp left to 'Roza's Gorge'. This detour will cost you 12km there and back.)

Return and head into **Mohos** (🚗), a pretty village in a fertile basin abounding with olive trees. Leave this village by heading diagonally across the square. A little way out of Mohos you'll have your first glimpse of the sea and a good view (☞) of the coastline and Stalida Beach below. There is a fairly awesome drop on one side of the road (edged with a crash barrier), so do drive carefully.

When you come to a roundabout on the A90 highway (85.5km), if you are pressed for time turn right here. Our main tour goes straight across, to the old main Iraklion/ Agios Nikolaos road at **Stalida** (87km 🚗). If you fancy a swim and some relaxation in the sun before heading back to base, sandy Anthoussa Beach is straight ahead.

But we head right here, to **Malia** ★ (92km ✝▲✕🚗⊕). You might like to visit the archaeological site some 2km beyond it, signposted off to the left. Some 1.5km past the turn-off to the site, you have another chance to join the 90 highway. If, instead, you want to visit Milatos, be sure to keep left on the old road at the Y-fork where right is signposted to Agios Nikolaos (via the A90 highway). The cave at **Milatos** (⌂🎒) was the setting in 1823 of a two-week siege in which over 3600 Cretans were massacred by the Turks. There is an ancient site nearby.

From Milatos continue (🚗 at 95km) through **Selinari** (101km ✝✕🚗WC). Walk 24 ends at the bus shelter just before the **Vrahasi** tunnel (102km) — remember to turn your lights off as you leave it. Then continue, homeward bound (🚗 at 113km, 115km), back to **Agios Nikolaos** (117km).

Car tour 8: A CENTRAL SWEEP

Agios Nikolaos • Hersonisos • Kasteli • Panagia • 'Embaros • Ano Viannos • Kato Symi • Ierapetra • Agios Nikolaos

See also photos on pages 16, 17, 92 and 147	Walks en route: Walks 9, 10, 12, 13, (19, 28, 29)
162km/100mi (without detours); 3h30min driving. All on main roads except for the 18km detour to the Viannos Omalos (4WD only).	Picnic suggestions: Kato Symi, (Viannos Omalos, Sarakina Gorge, Bramiana Reservoir, Vasikiki), Monastiraki

This excursion makes a great circling sweep that will ensure you see a good deal of Eastern Crete. For the most part we don't lead you off the beaten track on this tour, because there's plenty to see and do without straying far off good roads. An exception is the highly recommended detour halfway through the drive to the 'Viannos Omalos', only suitable if you are in a 4WD vehicle. Otherwise, this tour takes you past the start or finish of four walks, so there is ample opportunity to stretch your legs!

Leave Agios Nikolaos on the A90 highway for 'IRAKLIO'. At the major junction south of **Hersonisos** (38km ⛰✕🍴WC and outdoor **M** of Traditional Cretan Life), turn off right for 'KASTELI' and 'PLATEAU LASITHIOU' (road 92). At the round-about, follow the same signposting, to go back under the A90 and head south, soon passing Crete's only golf course. Roadworks between Hersonisos and Kasteli were in progress at time of writing, so keep following signs for 'KASTELI'.

Once in **Kasteli** (51km ⛽🍴), turn right at the first T-junction (for 'VIANNOS'). In the main square, turn left just in front of the taxi rank, then immediately right, with the pharmacy just to your right. These turns were *not signposted* at press date. The road climbs. After 300m you will need to take a *right* turn downhill: *not signed* when last checked, but ahead was signed 'Κεντρο' (Centre) and behind (the way we've just come) was signed to Iraklion.

Having left Kasteli behind, this road runs to the left of the aerodrome (where you ignore the

turning left to Agia Paraskevi). At 60km go straight over the roundabout ('VIANNOS 19') then keep left immediately for 'PANAGIA'. Four kilometres further on, at **Panagia** (64km), you will notice the mountains of the Dikti range unfolding before you — possibly still streaked with snow if it's early summer. Panagia is situated in a flat fertile basin, surrounded by clover-clad hills. There's a pretty view looking back over it at 66km (📷).

Pass the turn-off for 'Embaros, then drive through **Thomadiano**, where abundant water keeps the vegetation lush. Further on, keep straight on up the hill, ignoring signs for Martha, Pyrgos and Matala. Again keep straight on, ignoring signs for Chandros and Kastri, first descending gradually above **Kato Viannos** (81km 🍴) and then below **Ano Viannos** (84km ⛽✕🍴). By 88km, you'll be able to see down to the south coast — over the reddish-brown landscape dotted with green (📷). At **Amiras** (90km ✕) drive past two turnings right to Avri Beach and, next to the second, a striking memorial to the war dead.

Leaving Panagía, the Dikti mountains come into view — still snow-streaked in early May.

A kilometre past **Pefkos** (93km 🚌; the name means 'pine'), turn left up to **Kato Symi** ('ΚΑΤΟ ΣΨΜΙ'; 94km ✕) — a pretty, leafy village with both an heroic and tragic WWII history: Cretan rebels ambushed German troops, leaving about 100 dead; in retaliation — in addition to the usual executions — 11 villages were dynamited. There is a splendid opportunity for a picnic detour here: using the map recommended on page 12, drive up to the Minoan sanctuary of Hermes and Aphrodite (12km there and back). Water gushes out from hillside springs on the way up, so take a bottle with you to replenish your supply. But if you're in a 4WD vehicle, we'd suggest you go even further — to the 'Viannos Omalos' — a plateau 9km to the northwest, where you will find the cross-less church of Agía Pnevma, made out of the local purple slate and absolute tranquility for a picnic.

Back on the main road below Kato Symi (96km *without the detour*), turn left, eventually passing below blinding-white **Mournies** (105km ✕). One of our favourite hikes, Walk 28 shown on page 145, starts there and leads — via three gorges and masses of beautiful pines — to Males, higher up in the Dikti range. But since it's linear, we suggest a different version for motorists — Walk 29, which also takes in the Sarakina Gorge, the terrific picnic spot shown on pages 149 and 151. The tour continues along above Mirtos off to the right.

We now near the plastic greenhouses of the Ierapetra area, and we go through **Nea Anatoli** and **Gra Ligia**. You *can* get to the Bramiana Reservoir for Walk 19 or a picnic from here, but you might find it more straightforward to take the Kalamafka road from the large red-domed church just before **Ierapetra** (125km 🚐🏔✕🚌⊕MWC). Use the notes on page 18 to visit the town and then take the main north/south road past the start- or end-point of four walks and some good picnic spots, to return to **Agios Nikolaos** (162km).

Car tour 9: THE CRETAN COUNTRYSIDE

Agios Nikolaos • Kritsa • Kroustas • Kalo Horio • Agios Nikolaos

See also photos on pages 31, 58, 62-63, 64, 65, 66 and 67
45km/28mi; 1h15min driving — all on good roads.

Walks en route: Walks 1-5, 22
Picnic suggestions: Lato road at Kritsa, pine woods beyond Kroustas (20km along the tour)

Pine trees, pretty villages and lovely sea views are all on your doorstep if you're based in Agios Nikolaos — but you *do* have to know where to go. This drive makes a short sweep similar to the route of Walk 3 but, where we use roads today, the walk follows footpaths. Perhaps this foray deep into the countryside will tempt you to try some of our walks.

Leave Agios Nikolaos by following Car tour 6 on page 32 as far as **Kritsa★** (8km 🚻✕🚗). As you approach Kritsa, you'll pass a road off right to the lovely picnic setting shown on page 58 and the Dorian site of Lato (Walk 1, photo on page 57). Then carry on into the one-way

system and continue up into the village. Turn right as you meet the square, pass the bust of Rodante on your left and the church of Panagia Odigitria on the right. Then, at the Y-fork, turn left for '*KROUSTA/PRINA/ PLATEAU OF KATHARO*'. The road bends left (signed to Kroustas and

Prina), then quickly comes to a three-way junction where you go straight ahead (Car tour 6 goes right here). As you climb up out of Kritsa there's a good view (📷) of the hills in the Thripti range. After 11km you are really quite high up, looking straight onto Kritsa (📷).

Drive into **Kroustas** (13km ⚓✕) and keep going straight on through and out of the village. Walk 3 from Mardati brings you into Kroustas via the attractive back streets of this enchanting village. Drive beside a dry river bed and go over a bridge — this is where Walk 5 from Kalamafka comes in to Kroustas.

When the road divides (15km), take the left fork. From here on we follow a fairly new road, wide enough for two cars. But when we

first planned this drive, and even in previous editions of this book, it followed motorable — but exceedingly narrow — tracks and was not recommended for novice drivers or nervous passengers!

Keeping to the asphalt and ignoring all tracks right and left, you can enjoy the spectacular scenery. But do note a track off left after 4km, signed 'AGIOS IOANNIS 1KM'. You may like to take a detour to visit this tiny church. Keeping to the main road, about 1.5km further on, another track to the left (20km) heralds an area of lovely pine trees and woods, thick with oleander — a good picnic setting.

At 21km the road curves round sharply onto the next hill. Soon you will be able to see Kalo Horio, its valley and two bays, down to the left. This must be good bee and honey country, judging from the groups of hives that begin to appear as the pines run out and the olive groves begin.

When you come to the outskirts of **Prina**, turn left immediately — unless you want to go and look at the village — and go steeply downhill. After 200m this road makes a U-bend to the right and meets a road at a T-junction (24km): turn left here and soon you'll have a marvellous view of Kalo Horio spread out below you. The turquoise-blue water turns to deep sapphire as your gaze is drawn further out to sea.

The attractive cemetery in the foreground before **Pirgos** will catch your eye. Descend past the village, meet the north coast road below **Kalo Horio**, and turn left, back to **Agios Nikolaos** (45km).

Panagia Kera, near Kritsa — probably the most famous church in Eastern Crete

Car tour 10: KNOSSOS AND INLAND VILLAGES

Agios Nikolaos • (Iraklion) • Knossos • Arhanes • Vathypetro • Kasteli • Agios Nikolaos

162km/100mi; under 3h30min driving. Most of this tour is on good country roads. A stretch beyond Iraklion is narrow and requires patient driving if you're behind slow-moving traffic.
Walks en route: Walk 24
Picnic suggestion: Vathypetro

Plan on being out for most of the day, if you want to see Knossos, the museum of Iraklion and Vathypetro. This tour description omits Iraklion from the driving distances and times.

From Agios Nikolaos, take the main road to Iraklion (Exit A; Paleologou Street). Go straight ahead to the A90 highway at the traffic lights on the far side of town (ignoring the right turn to Iraklion by the old road). Keeping to the highway, you pass **Neapolis** and at 17km emerge from the **Vrahasi** tunnel where Walk 24 ends. Keep on past **Malia** and **Hersonisos**. Coming into **Iraklion**, go past the turn-off for 'Viannos/Port' and the industrial area (60km); keep ahead for 'IRAKLEIO 3'.

Two kilometres further on, at the next exit, go right for 'IRAKLEIO' and 'KNOSSOS'. Then, emerging from the highway underpass, *get in the left lane* and, opposite the petrol station (🚌), turn left for Knossos (*not* signposted at this point). You're now heading south on an attractive avenue (🚌) fringed with greenery, eventually signposted to 'KNOSSOS'. **Knossos★** (65km 🚌✗), the most famous site on Crete, was once the capital of the Minoan kingdom, as you may be aware.

After your visit, continue on the same main road past Knossos. Within a very short time you're in the depths of the countryside. Move on through olive groves and vines, proclaiming the industries of the region (🚌 at 69km). On the far side of **Patsides**, fork right for 'ARCHANES'. Come to **Kato Arhanes** (72km 🚌) and then fork right for 'CHOUDETSI', to skirt to the west of **Arhanes** (74km 🌳⛰). Carry on to the Minoan mansion, **Vathypetro★** (79km 🏛), a fine place to picnic, with wonderful views. Notable on its south side are the wine press

and ceramics kiln (16th century BC).

Once back on the main route, ignore small tracks going off at tangents. Three kilometres from Vathypetro, turn left into **Houdetsi** (82km 🌳🚌) and, on entering the village, keep round to the right for Iraklion (*not* signposted). The road passes **Agios Vasilios** (85km 🌳) and **Kaloni**. On the far side of Kaloni, just past the Peza wine-makers' co-operative (signed in Greek) and before a large fruit market, turn sharp right for 'KASTELLI' (87km; 🚌 not far past the turning). Go straight on through **Agios Paraskies** (🚌) then, leaving the village (90km), go straight over the crossroads.

The landscape changes as you climb higher into rockier, hilly countryside with cypresses. You may find that it's reminiscent, in places, of a country lane in Tuscany. Keep to the Kasteli road. Just before **Apostoli**'s large church (101km), you could make a short detour right to 'THRAPSANOS', one of the two villages in Crete specialising almost exclusively in pottery (the other is Margarites southeast of Rethimnon).

Outside the village the road, now lined with eucalyptus, leads on towards the brown and grey hills ahead, through **Kardoulianos** (🌳) and **Kasteli** (107km 🌳🚌). In the centre of Kasteli, opposite the taxi rank on the right, bear left (*not* signposted). Some 200 metres further on, turn left for 'HERSONISSOS/MALIA/IRAKLIO'. Now keep to this main road all the way to the A90 highway and then head east, back to **Agios Nikolaos** (162km).

Fresco at Knossos — the 'Priest-King'

Car tour 11: TO THE WEST

Agios Nikolaos • (Iraklion) • Rethimnon • Hania • Agios Nikolaos

404km/250mi; about 6 hours' driving there and back. The whole tour is generally good, main-road driving. Take care when there is a solid white line prohibiting overtaking; it's there for a reason. Even if you have wisely decided to stay overnight in Hania, we recommend that you head west in the morning — otherwise the mid-day sun will dazzle you, and you won't see a thing! Although this is a very long drive, you'll get value for money from your car — especially if driving is shared. As well as the map suggested on page 12, you may want to have the Terrain maps for Central Crete and Western Crete — as well as our own guide to Western Crete.

If you hire a car you'll be tempted, understandably, to drive west. The contrast between east and west is very marked, and this drive to Hania will impress upon you just how large Crete is. A great deal of the route is fringed by the sea, in its stunning shades of blue. As a backdrop there is the awe-inspiring Mount Ida and, further west, the White Mountains ('Levka Ori').

From Agios Nikolaos, take the main road to Iraklion (Exit A; Paleologou Street). Go straight ahead to the A90 highway at the traffic lights on the far side of town (ignoring the right turn to Iraklion by the old road). Keeping to the highway, bypass **Iraklion★** (63km 🚾❖⛰✕ 🚻⊕M).

Further along you pass the turn-off right for Fodele★ (88.5km ❖), El Greco's birthplace. The orange groves there, and the Byzantine church of Panagia, are attractions for visitors, but El Greco's reputed birthplace is a disappointment, having been extensively renovated and given over to tourism.

Staying on the oleander- and wild mimosa-lined road (now referring to the map of Western Crete), pass viewpoints over the sea and the upland countryside (📷 at 106, 108 and 109km; 🚻 at 110km). Around the 125km-mark, just before the Geropotamos Bridge, the White Mountains come into view. Even in summer they may be carrying a

mantle of snow on the peaks.

Keep to the A90 highway towards Rethimnon and either stay on the highway to bypass it or take the second exit if you want to visit this large pleasant town.

Rethimnon ★ (142km 🏛 ⛰ ✕ 🚰⊕**M**) has a good beach (down right, as you approach the centre of town). The old harbour is a nice place to stretch your legs. More than any other town on Crete, this still speaks of its medieval past, with its Ottoman and Venetian buildings. The museum is a very manageable size.

Once beyond the town (🚰 at 144km), the road rises, giving you good views back over Rethimnon's setting. Pass above the Gerani Cave ★ (150km ∩), situated below the bridge of the same name. Cross the Petres River — doubtless a dry bed leading to the sea. For the next 10km (🚰) the road runs straight along a sandy beach. If you decide to swim, take care — the currents are strong!

Driving into the 'county' of Hania, the mountains will be much more evident up to your left (📷 at 165km). Soon (169km), when

Hania is within striking distance, you could turn left to Vrises (✕), where spring water flows over the roadside and yoghurt flows out of bowls. Or you could turn right into the village of Georgioupoli (⛰ ✕) and have a swim. Pressing on to Hania (🚰 at 171km), there are excellent views above the Souda naval base.

At 196km leave the A90 highway by turning right for 'CHANIA/SOUDA' and, at the following junction, just 1km further on, turn left for 'CHANIA'. Now a busy narrow road (🚰) — keep straight on; don't follow the arrow pointing right, back to Souda — takes you into the town. A one-way system begins by the statue of a *kri-kri* (ibex). Continue by taking the right-hand fork. You are in the main street, Tzanakaki, which will lead you past the public gardens and to the market in **Hania** ★ (202km 🏛 ✝ ⛰ ✕ 🚰⊕**M**).

Perhaps this attractive town will entice you to return to Crete, make your base here, and explore the west, using *Landscapes of Western Crete*.

Venetian harbour at Rethimnon

☀ Walking

We have covered a lot of ground putting these walks together, and we're sure you'll be surprised and delighted to discover so many varied landscapes in Eastern Crete. When people think of walking on Crete, they invariably imagine the White Mountains and the Samaria Gorge — Western Crete. Frankly, we're delighted that the east of the island — despite catering for tourists — still has miles and miles of 'hidden' landscapes awaiting your discovery.

The 'Landscapes' series is built around walks and excursions that can be made *in day trips* from your home base, even if you choose not to hire a car. So all the walks in this book were originally conceived as day excursions *accessible by bus* from Agios Nikolaos. These days many people are keen to hire cars and often prefer circular walks. We have tried to cater for that in this edition, but do bear in mind that the beautiful old donkey trails *(kalderimi)* were built to take villagers from one place to another: they are all linear. A good solution is to walk from A to B and take a bus back to your car — or, to be on the safe side, drive to the end of the walk, leave your car there, and take a bus back to the start. Suitable walks (not necessarily circular) are indicated by a ⊜ symbol in the Contents. It may be one of the *variations* of the main walk that is recommended: look for the 🚗 symbol under 'Access' (with waypoints for the walk start so that you can set your satnav).

Do consider combining some of the walks. We've indicated where routes overlap on the walking and touring maps. But *never try to get from one walk to another on uncharted terrain!* Only link up walks by following paths described in these notes or by using roads or tracks; don't try to cross rough country (which might be dangerous) or private land (where you might not have the right of way).

The people you meet are very much a part of the landscape, countryside and essence of Crete. Do greet anyone you pass or see working in a field when you are out walking. Please don't — perhaps through your natural reserve — pretend they don't exist!

There are walks in this book for everyone.

Beginners: Start on the walks graded ● or ●, and check all the short and alternative walks — *and the picnics!*

Experienced walkers: If you are accustomed to rough

terrain and are feeling fit, you should be able to enjoy all our walks. Many — especially those in gorges — require agility, and a couple will demand a head for heights as well. Take into account the season and weather conditions: don't attempt the more strenuous walks in high summer; protect yourself from the sun and carry ample water.

Experts: Most of the walks that attract you will be found in *Landscapes of Western Crete*. It's unlikely that you will find any of the walks in the east really challenge you, so relax and simply enjoy the wonderful scenery.

Grading, waymarking, maps, GPS

We've tried to give you a quick overview of each walk's **grade** in the Contents. But many of our walks have shorter or alternative versions! In the Contents we've only had space to show the *lowest* grade of a *main* walk: for full details, including easier versions, see the walk itself. Here is a brief overview of the four gradings:

● very easy — more or less level (perhaps with a short climb to a viewpoint); good surfaces underfoot; easily followed

● easy-moderate — ascents/descents of no more than about 300-500m/1000-1800ft; good surfaces underfoot; easily followed

● moderate-strenuous — ascents/descents may be over 500m/1800ft; variable surfaces underfoot — you must be sure-footed and agile

● expert — only suitable for very experienced hillwalkers with a head for heights; hazards may include landslides or balancing on ledges with no respite from constant exposure. (This last grade only applies to walks described in *Landscapes of Western Crete*.)

Any of the above grades may be followed by:

: *danger* of vertigo; the walk demands a good head for heights

Assigning grades to walks is *very* subjective — and giving them a 'vertigo' rating even more so! Until you get used to Crete's terrain and know your 'vertigo tolerance', why not try walking with one of the many **guided groups**? Note also: should you wish to walk further afield (perhaps climb Mount Ida), we suggest you contact the Alpine Club in Iraklion (53, Dikaiosynis Street; telephone 2810 227609). They arrange guided trips and overnight stays.

It's always encouraging to see **waymarking** along the route. But, unless we specifically advise you to follow it, don't *rely* on waymarking. You will certainly come across parts of the 'E4' network of long-distance routes. These 'European Rambler Trails' are usually well waymarked with yellow paint and sign-posted with yellow and black triangular plaques (see photo on page 23). If a walk in this book has become part of the E4, we mention this and show the route on the walking map — but the

E4 is growing all the time, so we may be a bit out of date! (The entire **E4 trail across Crete** is shown on our touring maps, but there is a wealth of helpful information on the web.)

The **maps** in this book are based on Openstreetmap mapping (see page 2), but have been very heavily annotated from our notes and GPS work in the field. We hope that these maps, which we have found to be *very* accurate on the ground, will be a boon to walkers. It is a pity that we have to reproduce them at only 1:50,000 to keep the book to a manageable size; quite a few walkers buy both the paperback *and* download our pdf files so that they can enlarge the maps — or you can enlarge them on a colour photocopier. Otherwise, we recommend the widely available GPS-compatible Anavasi 1:25,000 maps.

Free **GPS track** downloads and **height profiles** are available for all our walks: see the Eastern Crete page on the Sunflower website. Please bear in mind, however, that GPS readings should *never* be relied upon as your sole reference point, as conditions can change overnight. *But even if you don't use GPS*, our maps are now so accurate that you can easily compare them with Google Maps on your smartphone and pinpoint your exact position. And it's great fun opening our GPX files in Google Earth to preview the walks in advance!

Things that bite or sting

Dogs on Crete, in our experience, are full of bravado, but not vicious. They bark like fury — indeed, what would be the point of guarding livestock if they did not? — and they will approach you, seemingly full of evil intention. However, they will shy off if you continue unperturbed. 'El-la' is a useful word to know. It means 'come here', if spoken encouragingly, or 'come

You will see many, many beehives on the island — be sure to carry your medication if you are allergic to bee stings!

off it', when said in a slightly diffident tone. Use it encouragingly with the dogs, and they'll soon go away. If you carry a walking stick, keep it out of sight and don't use it threateningly. If dogs worry you, you may like to invest in a 'Dog Dazer' — an ultra-sonic device which deters threatening dogs without harming them. These are widely available on the web.

In the autumn you may be startled by gunfire, but it's only **hunters** — invariably on Sundays and holidays — in pursuit of game. You'll doubtless see them dropping or throwing stones into bushes — Greek beating!

Have respect for **donkeys**' hind legs; it's highly unlikely they'll kick, but don't forget the possibility.

Snakes may be seen, and vipers have been identified on Crete, but they keep a very low profile and are not widespread. Poisonous **spiders**, called 'rogalida', do exist on the island, but it's highly unlikely you'll even catch a glimpse of one, as they are burrowers. You're more likely to see **scorpions**; they are harmless, but their sting is painful. Like spiders and snakes, they are likely to be hiding under rocks and logs in the daytime hours. So if you move a rock, etc, to sit down, just have a look under it first.

People who are allergic to bee stings should always carry their medication. **Bees** abound in summer, especially around water troughs and thyme bushes.

Although we've mentioned this collection of creatures, it's very doubtful indeed that you will encounter anything that would harm you.

What to take

If you're already on Crete when you find this book, and you haven't any special equipment such as a rucksack or walking boots, you can still do many of the walks — or you can buy the basic equipment at one of the sports shops in Agios Nikolaos or Iraklion. Don't attempt the more difficult walks without the proper gear. For each walk in the book, the *minimum* equipment is listed. Above all, you need thick-soled stout walking trainers or walking boots. *Ankle support* is advisable in your footwear — indeed *essential* on many of the walks, where the path descends steeply over loose stones. You may find the following checklist useful:

walking trainers or walking boots
long trousers, tight at the ankles
long-sleeved shirt (sun protection)
waterproof rain gear
telescopic walking stick(s)
smartphone (**112 is the Europe-wide emergency number**)

up-to-date bus timetable
windproof (zip opening)
bandages and plasters
extra pair of (long) socks
knives and openers
light jerseys (or similar)
antiseptic cream

water bottle, paper plates, etc
tissues
sunhat, sunglasses, sun cream
groundsheet

whistle, torch, compass/gps
spare bootlaces
small rucksack
insect repellent

Please bear in mind that we've not done *every* walk in this book under *all* conditions. We might not realise, for example, just how hot or how exposed some walks might be. Beware of the sun and the effects of dehydration. Don't be deceived by cloud cover: you can still get sunburnt, especially on the back of your neck and legs. We rely on your good judgement to modify the 'equipment' list at the start of each walk according to the season.

Where to stay

We have used Agios Nikolaos as our walking base, since the majority of people stay there when visiting Eastern Crete. Due to the size of the island, some of the walks require changing buses or driving considerable distances. Although this makes the day longer, it has the advantage that you see more of the countryside. There are no organised facilities for overnight stays in the mountains in Eastern Crete, but if you'd like to stay in a mountain village overnight, it's worth asking for a bed for the night. The shepherd community at Katharon above Kritsa, for example, has been known to provide pleasant — although very basic — shelter for the night. Enquire about renting a bed for the night at tavernas and *cafeneions*.

If you're staying at a base other than Agios Nikolaos, the walks are still possible — but bus users should check the time-tables on pages 157-158 to make sure that the walks furthest away from your base are practicable.

Walkers' checklist

The following points cannot be stressed too often:
- **At any time a walk may become unsafe** due to storm damage or bulldozing. If the route is not as described in this book, and your way ahead is not secure, do not attempt to continue.
- **Never walk alone** — four is the best walking group.
- **Transport** connections at the end of a walk may be vital.
- Proper **footwear** is essential.
- **Warm clothing** is needed in the mountains; even in summer, take something appropriate with you, in case you are delayed.
- **Mobile/smartphone, compass/gps, torch, whistle** weigh little, but might save your life.
- **Extra food** and drink should be taken on long walks.

Many of the walks pass threshing floors, where you may see oxen threshing wheat (as here at Kato Pines, Walk 8)

■ Always take a **sunhat** with you, and in summer a cover-up for your arms and legs as well.
■ A **stout stick** or **telescopic walking stick** is a help on rough terrain and to discourage the rare unfriendly dog.
■ Read and reread the **important note** on page 2 and the Country code on page 11, as well as guidelines on grade and equipment for each walk you plan to do.

Weather

April, May, September and October are perhaps the best months to walk on Crete. The air temperature is moderate, but the sun shines. It is possible to walk during June, July and August, however, because although it may be very hot by the coast, there's often a light breeze in the mountains. There's no doubt it's more tiring though, and great care should be taken in the sun and heat. The *meltemi* blowing in from the north tends to be a bad-tempered wind, bringing strong, hot breezes in the height of summer. These breezes stir up the dust, move the air about, but don't really cool it.

During February and November it often rains. The months of December and January are chilly and, if it rains, it may do so for two or three days at a time. However, the winter in Crete brings an incredible clarity on sunny days and some really perfect walking weather, when temperatures may be around 20°C (68°F).

It's worth remarking, too, that more often than not, when it's windy along the north coast, it's calm on the south of the island.

Greek for walkers

In the major tourist areas you hardly need to know any Greek at all but, once you are out in the countryside, a few words of the language will be helpful. Anyhow, it's nice to be able to communicate — if only a little — and people will marvel at your attempts.

Here's one way to ask directions in Greek *and understand the answers you get!* First memorise the few 'key' questions given below. Then, always follow up your key question with a **second question demanding a yes (ne) or no (ochi) answer.** (By the way, Greeks invariably raise their heads to say 'no', which looks to us like the beginning of a 'yes'. And 'ochi' (no) might be pronounced as **o**-hee, **o**-shee or even **oi**-ee.)

Following are the two most likely situations in which you may have to use some Greek. The dots (...) show where you will fill in the name of your destination. The approximate pronunciation of place names is in the Index.

■ Asking the way

The key questions

English	Approximate Greek pronunciation
Good day, greetings (formal)	**Hair**-i-tay
Hello, hi (informal)	**Yas**-sas (plural); **Yia**-soo (singular)
Good morning/afternoon	Kah-lee-**may**-rah/Kah-lee-**spay**-rah
Please —	**Sas** pa-ra-ka-**loh** —
where is	**pou ee**-nay
the road that goes to ... ?	o **thro**-mo stoh ... ?
the footpath that goes to ... ?	ee mo-no-**pa**-ti stoh ... ?
the bus stop?	ee **sta**-ssis?
Many thanks.	Eff-hah-ree-**stoh** po-**li**.

Secondary question leading to a yes/no answer

English	Approximate Greek pronunciation
Is it here?	**Ee**-nay **etho**?
Is it there?	**Ee**-nay eh-**kee**?
Is it straight ahead?	**Ee**-nay kat-eff-**thia**?
Is it behind?	**Ee**-nay **pee**-so?
Is it to the right?	**Ee**-nay thex-**ya**?
Is it to the left?	**Ee**-nay aris-teh-**rah**?
Is it above?	**Ee**-nay eh-**pano**?
Is it below?	**Ee**-nay **kah**-to?

■ Asking a taxi driver to take you somewhere and return for you, or asking him to collect you somewhere

English	Approximate Greek pronunciation
Please —	**Sas** pa-ra-ka-**loh** —
would you take us to ... ?	tha **pah**-reh mas stoh ... ?
Come and pick us up	**El**-la na mas **pah**-reh-teh
from ... (place) at ... (time)*	apo ... stees ...*

Instead of memorising the hours of the day, simply point out on your watch the time you wish to be collected.

As you may need a taxi for some walks, why not ask your tour rep or hotel reception to find a driver who speaks English (many now do). We'd also recommend that you use an inexpensive phrase book with easily-understood pronunciation hints, as well as a good selection of useful phrases.

By the way: it's unlikely that a map will mean anything to the *older* people you may meet en route. Doubtless, they will ask you '**Pooh pah**-tay?' — at the same time turning a hand over in the air, questioningly. It means 'Where are you going?', and quite a good answer is 'Stah voo-**na**', which means 'to the mountains'.

Organisation of the walks

The 30 main walks in this book are located in the parts of Eastern Crete most easily accessible by public transport, using Agios Nikolaos as the base. We hope that even if you're staying somewhere else in the east, most will be within range — especially if you've hired a car. We've also included details about the famous Samaria Gorge walk in Western Crete (Walk 31), which is a popular excursion from Agios Nikolaos — and one that many of you will no doubt want to do!

The book is set out so that you can plan walks easily — depending on how far you want to go, your abilities and equipment — and what time you are willing to get up in the

Late spring on the Katharon Plateau (Car tour 6)

In the Orno Mountains (Walk 11)

morning! You might begin by considering the fold-out touring map inside the back cover of the book. Here you can see at a glance the overall terrain, the road network, and the general orientation of the walking maps in the text. Quickly flipping through the book, you'll find that there's at least one photograph for each walk.

Having selected one or two potential excursions from the map and the photographs, look over the planning information at the beginning of each walk description. Here you'll find distance/hours, grade, equipment, and access. If the walk sounds beyond your ability or fitness, check to see if there's a shorter or alternative version. We've tried to provide walking opportunities less demanding of agility wherever possible.

When you are on your walk, you will find that the text begins with a general introduction and then quickly turns to a detailed description of the route itself. As well as distances, *times* are given for reaching certain points in the walk. Once you've done one walk, you'll be able to compare our very steady pace with your own; we hope you'll find we're in step, give or take! *Note that our times do not include any stops, so do allow for them.*

Below is a key to the symbols used on our walking maps.

main road	E4 long-distance hiking route	start.waypoint
secondary road	church, monastery. chapel	windmill.wind turbine
4WD track	cemetery.shrine	pylon.aerial
rough track	factory	picnic spot (see page 10)
footpath	bus stop.parking	best views
route of main walk and direction	spring, tank etc	page reference: map continuation
alternative route	ancient site	watermill.cave
other described walk		

See also photos on pages 31, 40-41, 58 and 64

NB: Lato is *closed on Mondays,* otherwise open daily from 08.30-15.00 (19.30 in summer); small entry fee
Distance: 15km/9.3mi; 5h15min, plus time to visit the site
Grade: ● moderate-strenuous on account of length; height difference of about 350m/1150ft
Equipment: walking trainers (boots if returning via the gorge), sunhat, picnic, water
Picnic: at Lato or at a chapel on the west side of the Lato road (fine view to Kritsa shown on page 58)
Access: ⛟ to/from Kritsa — or ⛟ (Timetable 3; journey time 15min). By car, park in the free car park on the right, just past the signposted right turn to Lato (35° 9.445'N, 25° 38.798'E).

Alternative walks

1 Kritsa — Lato — Kritsa (9km/5.6mi; 2h15min, plus time to visit the site). ● Easy; height difference of about 100m/330ft. Equipment/access as main walk. Follow the main walk to Lato, then return along the road, past a chapel on the right (recommended picnic spot). Perhaps make a diversion to Panagia Kera, the church shown on pages 40-41 (see map).

2 Kritsa — Lato — Hamilo (8.7km/5.4mi; 2h15min, plus time to visit the site). ● Easy gradual

ascent; the descent of 250m/820ft is stony and somewhat steeper. Equipment and access by ⛟ (as main walk); return by ⛟ from Hamilo (not in the timetables): departs 15.00 *weekdays only;* journey time 10min. Follow the main walk to Lato (**❺**), and walk back down the asphalt road to the SHRINE (**ⓐ**). Then take the path opposite it. This very stony donkey trail zigzags down in great steps beside a shrub-clothed ravine, which is quite unexpected and makes a picturesque contrast to the Lasithi mountains beyond. Thirty minutes from Lato (**1h45min**), you meet a lane. Follow it to the right but after just 50m/yds take a track to the right (**ⓑ**; by some TRANSFORMERS). After 250m/yds, fork left. In five minutes (350m), at another fork, branch off right. You're on the fertile plain of Lakonia, covered with olive trees. Ignore a turning to the right (**2h**). Two minutes later you've almost come to the main road; take the lane to the right, just before the road. In another two minutes, turn left at a T-junction. Five minutes more and you're on the main Lakonia road. Turn right and come into pretty **Hamilo** (**ⓒ**; **2h15min**), where you'll doubtless be pleased to see two tavernas. The BUS STOP is opposite the CHURCH.

Hⁱere's a good introduction to the hills around Agios Nikolaos: after each range yet another summit comes into view and then fades into the distance. This is also a pleasant way to visit the ancient Dorian site at Lato, avoiding the asphalt road.

Either leave the car in the car park or take the bus to where it turns round in **Kritsa** (**⭕**). Then **start out** by walking uphill into the village along the main street, passing the big church of **Panagia Odigitria** on your right, opposite a *cafeneion* and

TAXI RANK. At the fork at the top of the road turn right (left goes to Kroustas) and continue along this shop-lined road, passing a small square filled with café tables and chairs. After 200m/yds, when you come to a three-way fork, take the middle route — a small concrete village road. (The route to the left is signposted to Katharon; to the right are steps leading downhill.) After another 200m, at the end of the road, keep right downhill at a telegraph pole. Ignore any turnings left or right. Arriving at the large church of **Agios Georgios**, walk across the front of it and bend down to the right just after it, on concrete steps. The concrete gives way to cobbles; this was an old donkey trail.

Very soon you're at the edge of the village with views to the Dikti range in the distance. At the bottom of the cobbled steps, turn right and head diagonally across a road, to pick up a donkey trail on the far side. This takes you steeply downhill; take care, it's slithery! The cobbles become a rough track which takes

you onto a concrete village road. At the bottom of this road, go left on the asphalt road to Lato. Follow this road round, past a sign to Lato, and cross over an old BRIDGE (**❶**; **20min**). Turn left immediately after the bridge on a motorable track heading towards the Kritsa Gorge (SIGNPOSTED 'TO THE GORGE').

Some 350m/yds along, as you pass two CONCRETED CISTERNS and an orange water pump on the right (**25min**), you could make a diversion down into the Kritsa Gorge (**❷**; see Walk 2) by turning left — as indicated by a small signpost. The main walk turns right uphill here on a stony track, to continue towards Lato. Four to five minutes from this junction (after 250m/yds), on the brow of the hill, take the much narrower donkey trail

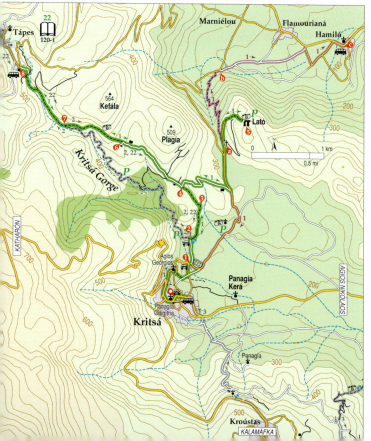

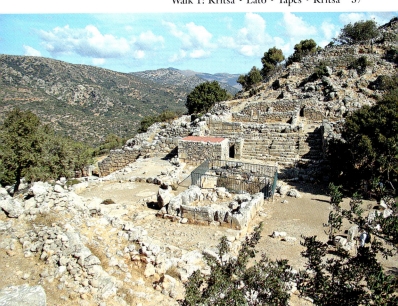

Lato

going up to the left. *Watch out,* after just over 250m, when you are on level ground again (**35min**), and follow the trail carefully as it makes a wide bend up to the left (**❸**); it's easy to miss this bend, as it looks as if a path goes straight ahead at this point. The donkey trail runs alongside a wall and then continues with walls either side.

Not far beyond a wire-mesh fence (please refasten it after passing) the donkey trail peters out at a ROUGH MOTORABLE TRACK (**❹**; **40min**). Here turn right for Lato. (After your visit to Lato you will return to this track and follow it in the other direction, to make for Tapes.)

Walk for 800m/half a mile and, when you meet the asphalt road, turn left. At the Y-fork, head right for Lato. After less than 200m you pass a small trail off left, opposite a SHRINE (**ⓐ**). *(Alternative walk 2 takes*

this trail on the way down to Hamilo.) Keep straight on up the road to the **Lato** SITE (**❺**; **1h15min**). The Dorians chose a delightful setting, with wonderful views over almond and olive trees down to their harbour at Agios Nikolaos and the splendid Mirabello Gulf.

Once you've rambled round the site, go back to where you joined the motorable track at the 40min-point (**❹**; **1h50min**).

Now carry on straight uphill, passing a breeze-block and concrete building with double gates (on the left; **2h**). Take the first right fork after this farm building and ignore a track going off to the right almost immediately. Pass a fenced-off, large breeze-block building up to the right (**2h10min**). (There may be dogs around here.) A few minutes later, pass through a wire gate — closing it behind you. Continue along the track, keeping the wire fence on the

Kritsa from the road to Lato — a lovely shady picnic setting

left and moving gradually uphill.
Very shortly after the wire gate, the
track bends left to a small building.
Keep straight ahead here on a path
(**6**; an OLD DONKEY TRAIL — you'll
sometimes spot cobbles underfoot).
There is fencing to your left, then a
stone wall. The path starts to run
high up (but not vertiginously so)
along the right-hand side of the river
valley, then goes gently downhill. At
some point you will notice the
houses of Tapes up ahead in the
distance.

Under 1km along, you merge
with the main path in the **Kritsa
Gorge** (**7**; **2h30min**) — just before
the route in the gorge itself is
blocked off. Head right uphill here.
In five minutes you catch a glimpse
of Tapes up ahead and then pass
through a GATE. Shortly afterwards,
the now-stony trail (marked with
CAIRNS and very sporadic BLUE DOTS)
leads up left from the bed of this
tributary stream. Within a few
minutes it crosses the stream bed
again. You pass through a MESH GATE

(perhaps with hard-to-find
fastenings) and almost immediately
cross the stream bed. Half a minute
later, cross the stream bed again and
go up into an olive grove on your
left. Follow occasional waymarking
up the terraces. Continue diagonally
uphill, passing to the left of a WATER
TROUGH (**2h45min**). From here you
can see your route ahead — a small
earthen path, strewn with stones,
that winds steeply uphill. (Having
seen the houses of Tapes earlier, you
will know where you are heading.)

It's a good five- to eight-minute
climb to the outskirts of **Tapes**.
When you reach the edge of the
hamlet, curve left on concrete and,
two minutes later, come to a
cafeneion with spiral staircase (**8**;
3h). From here return to **Kritsa** (**O**;
5h). The route is described in Walk
22 on page 122, starting at the
4h10min-point. Or go back via the
gorge, if you're well shod and still
full of energy.

Walk 2: KRITSA GORGE

See also photos on pages 31, 40-41, 58 and 64
Distance: 7km/4.3mi; 2h45min (add 40min if travelling by bus or parking in Kritsa's car park)
Grade: ● moderate, with a height difference of 250m/820ft; agility is required for scrambling up and jumping down boulders.
Equipment: walking boots, long trousers, sunhat, water, picnic
Picnic: anywhere in the gorge
Access: 🚌 to/from Kritsa — or 🚐 (Timetable 3; journey time 15min).

Travelling by car, you could park in the free car park on the right, just past the signposted road to Lato. *But our timings start* from this Lato road: turn right for Lato as you arrive at Kritsa, just in front of the cypress-studded cemetery. Park 500m along, just before a small bridge on a U-bend (35° 9.655'N, 25° 38.907'E), beyond which there is a sign for Lato (straight on) and the Kritsa Gorge (left). (There is also some parking along the left turn to the gorge, just before the track ends.)

A very accessible, small, but splendid gorge makes Kritsa an excellent hub not only for shopping, site-visiting, and hill-village exploring, but for walking off the beaten track as well.

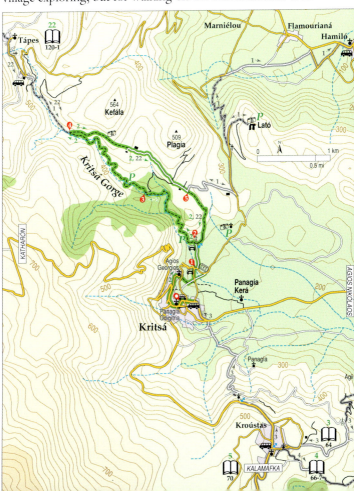

To **start the walk** from the BUS STOP OR CAR PARK in **Kritsa** (⊙) follow Walk 1 (page 50) to the old BRIDGE (❶; **20min**). Alternatively, if you park by the bridge *(where our timings start)*, head left on the rough motor track just past the bridge (where a road sign to the right indicates 'Lato' and there's a hand-painted sign on the left, '*TO THE GORGE*'. You can see the gorge countryside immediately, straight ahead. Some 350m/yds off the road, you're likely to see cars parked by a large POWER PYLON and

In the Kritsa Gorge

a *WATER PUMP/CISTERNS*. Turn left here down towards the river bed; there's another signpost *'TO THE GORGE'* (❷; **5min**). In a minute you're amongst big, smooth boulders and stones — and a good amount of shade. Anywhere past here is lovely for picnicking.

A description of the gorge walk itself is superfluous: there are plenty of *CAIRNS* and *ARROWS* in the river bed to show you the best way past the 'dead ends', and several times you'll find *METAL RUNGS* to help you over particularly imposing boulders. Before long (**20min**) the gorge is at its narrowest. There are some spectacular 'funnel'-like passages where the gorge walls rear up beside you — sometimes as much as 150m/500ft. It's refreshingly cool.

After you have passed through the gorge, the river bed opens out slightly (**35min**). When you reach a T-junction of sorts, head round to the right. Soon (**1h05min**) a *NETTING FENCE* running across the river bed may bar the way, although it is usually trampelled down. Cairns will indicate the best way round it, as you do need to carry straight on in the river bed. Just past here, a *SIGN POINTS AHEAD TO TAPES*, and a wide path heads off right, up and out of the river bed (❸; a possible short-cut). At another *NETTING FENCE* across a narrower section of river bed (**1h20min**), you should find an opening on the right. There are plenty of *CAIRNS* on the far side to encourage you! Following the bends of the river bed, within 10 minutes you come to another *FENCE* with a *CAIRN* beyond it (**1h30min**); again, you should find an opening on the right.

Keep looking over to the right, and you should see a path halfway up the hillside, beneath the rock face; it's your return route to Kritsa.

Shortly after spotting that path, another *FENCE BARS THE WAY ALONG THE RIVER BED* (45min from the sign for 'Tapes'; **1h50min**). Just before the fence, turn *sharp right* on path supported by stone walls (❹; straight on leads to Tapes; Walks 1 and 15).

As this path leads uphill to the right, bits of cobbles come underfoot — it's an old donkey trail. After ten minutes, at the top of the rise, you can see the sea at Kalo Horio. Follow the cairn-marked rocky path, more or less alongside a wall with a fence on top, and heading in the direction of a large farm building. Some 25 minutes along the path you come onto a motorable track (**2h15min**). Ten minutes later continue straight ahead, ignoring a track going back off to the left. Within half a minute go left at a slanting T-junction, to pass a *STONE BUILDING WITH DOUBLE GATES* on your right. Continue straight on, ignoring a track going off to the left (behind which you can see the Lato road). Then, just where the track you are on bends to the left, go straight ahead on a *DONKEY TRAIL* (❺), keeping the fencing on your right. After two-three minutes follow the donkey trail in a hard bend to the left and then a hard bend back round to the right. Almost immediately the first houses of Kritsa come into view (**2h30min**).

When the path comes down onto a track, head right towards Kritsa. Five minutes later you come to the track with the large *POWER PYLON* and pass the path you took down into the gorge at the start of the walk (❷; **2h40min**). Turn left, back to the Lato road, then go right, over the *BRIDGE*, back to your car (❶; **2h45min**). Allow another 20-25min to retrace your steps to Kritsa (◉), if you came by bus or parked there.

Walk 3: MARDATI • KROUSTAS • KRITSA

More photos on pages 31, 65, 67
Distance: 8km/5mi; 2h35min
Grade: ● moderate, with a height difference of 350m/1150ft. Shady
Equipment: walking trainers, long trousers, sunhat, water, picnic
Picnic: north of Agii Apostoli
Access: 🚐 to Mardati (Kritsa bus, Timetable 3); journey time under 10min. Or 🚗; park near the start of the walk/bus stop (35° 9.660'N, 25° 41.155'E). Return on the 🚐 same bus from Kritsa — back to Mardati for your car, or back to base. Or leave your car at Kritsa and take the

bus to Mardati to start out. The (free) Kritsa car park is on the right, just past the signposted road off right to Lato

Short walk: Mardati to Kroustas
(4.5km/2.8mi; 1h 30min). ●
Moderate ascent of 350m/1150ft. Equipment as above. Access by 🚐 as main walk; return from Kroustas (not in the timetables): buses depart 14.50 (Mon-Fri), 16.35 (Sat); no Sunday buses. Follow the main walk to Kroustas (❸). The bus stops where the road widens out, by the fountain shown on page 67.

Not far from Agios Nikolaos, this is a good morning's outing with pleasant rewards. A modicum of effort will take you via deep countryside and the enchanting village of Kroustas, then almost in a circle to Kritsa.

Get off the bus (or park) by the few houses of **Mardati** (⬤). **Start out** by continuing along the road towards Kritsa. Pass a SHRINE on the left and, 120m/ yds further on, turn left down a TRACK (**❶**; **5min**) through olive groves and pastureland. Two minutes along, come to a T-junction: turn left and then immediately right, now on a

motorable track. Almost at once, take the fork to the right. Go straight over a crossing track (**12min**). Once over a river bed, follow the track uphill. After two minutes you'll have a lovely view of Kritsa on your right, perfect for a picnic. Two minutes further uphill are some OLD MILLS (**❷**), one of them now used to store grain, while up ahead the church of Agii Apostoli is hidden in vegetation. Cross over another track and carry straight on uphill to a Y-fork, where you head right.

Go straight over another crossing track (**30min**), where the church of **Agii Apostoli** (**❸**) is off to the left. The track, now very eroded, heads left after 75m. Again, keep straight uphill on a narrower track. When this starts to descend to the right, be sure to locate a faint blue arrow on a rock. It points you left up a steep narrow path — overgrown, winding and stony. There are faint blue paint marks at a few crucial junctions, but just follow the hunters' spent cartridges! Past a WATER TROUGH, you enjoy good views back to Agios Nikolaos. Eventually the path winds up to a T-JUNCTION with a track (**❹**). Follow the track to the left, then ignore three turnings to the left. Rising to a wider track at another T-JUNCTION (**❺**; **55min**), turn left; a TRANSMITTER is just above you. Kritsa can be seen off to the right. Beyond and to the right, in the distance, lies the village of Tapes (Walk 15). Having followed the wide track round the hill with the TRANSMITTER, you can see Kalo

Kroustas

Horio, setting for Walk 4, and the beautiful hills beyond it (**1h**). When the track splits, keep right and uphill. Round another bend, the church at

Kritsa spice shop

Kroustas comes into view (**1h10min**). Just past a track off right to a farm building, at a T-junction, turn left. Soon you're in the back streets of **Kroustas**. Wend your way towards the centre, keeping left at the next few forks and passing to the right of a tiny CHURCH. Go left at the fork just past

64

this church, then turn right and right again. You come to the FOUNTAIN shown on page 67, on the right, and the main road (**6**; **1h25min**).

Turn right here and walk downhill towards Kritsa. In about 10 minutes, turn right down a concrete track between railings, passing a FOUNTAIN in a paved area under a large hollyoak and plane tree and then a CHAPEL on the right (**7**; **1h40min**). Dark red dot waymarks mark an old stone-laid but overgrown path at the left of the chapel: within a few minutes this deposits you on an earthen track. Turn left downhill; then, a minute later, at a T-junction, turn right.

Continue for about 12-13 minutes to a FOUR-WAY JUNCTION (**8**), where you turn left downhill towards Kritsa. At the T-junction six minutes later, turn left on a track which soon crosses a watercourse (likely to be dry in summer). Head uphill and, at the next junction, go right towards Kritsa. Ignore a concrete track to the right almost at once and, at the next junction, go right and cross a bridge. You meet the main road near the exit from Kritsa's one-way system (55min from Kroustas; **1h20min**). Follow it for 15 minutes to BUS STOP in the centre of **Kritsa** (**9**; **2h35min**).

Walk 4: FROM KROUSTAS TO KALO HORIO

See also photo on pages 62-63
Distance: 8km/5mi; 2h40min (add 2km/40min return to the beach)
Grade: ● moderate descent of 520m/1700ft; the path at the 35min-point is steep — good underfoot, but slippery after rain
Equipment: walking trainers, sunhat, water, picnic, swimwear
Picnic: at Agios Nikolaos chapel
Access: 🚌 to Kroustas (not in the timetables): buses depart 07.00 (Mon-Sat), 14.30 (Mon-Fri), 16.15

(Sat); journey time less than 10min; no Sunday buses. Return on 🚌 from Kalo Horio (Timetables 5, 6, 8); journey time 20min
Alternative walk: Mardati — Kroustas —Kalo Horio (13km/8mi; 4h10min). ● Moderate-strenuous; ascent of over 300m/1000ft and long descent of 520m/1700ft. Combine this with Walk 3 (●): take a 🚌 to Mardati (see page 62) to start.

This walk, almost all downhill, takes you from the charming village of Kroustas to the sparkling sea. For those who want a more demanding day out, it combines perfectly with Walk 3 — you'll have earned your swim when you reach Kalo Horio!

Start out facing the CHURCH in the pretty village of **Kroustas** (⭕). Walk north (towards Kritsa) for 100m/yds, then turn right into an alley with a FOUNTAIN on the left. Ignore a turning right, then just keep straight ahead for 120m, until the alley turns sharp left towards a small CHURCH. Keep straight ahead here, heading south downhill out of Kroustas on a wide concreted path. As it curves round through plots, the landscape changes quite noticeably. As you leave, look back at Kroustas, sheltering behind a huge buttress of rock.

When the path meets a concrete track, keep left downhill (in the same direction). Soon the track becomes earthen underfoot. A bit under 1km along the track makes a pronounced U-bend to the left (❶; **35min**). Take the path going right here (by a high CAIRN). This old cobbled path, waymarked with faded blue paint blobs (and some newer deep red ones), leads down into a small GORGE. *Note:* it's steep, narrow and sometimes covered with loose stones. You soon cross over the

Kroustas church, where the walk starts

largish stones in the river bed, then head up the other side.

Cross the BROW OF THE HILL (❷; **1h**). Spectacular views await you: first over Agios Nikolaos and then, a little further on, over Kalo Horio, nestling in a basin surrounded by hills, open on one side to the sea. You may notice the

65

occasional paint blob on rocks —
reassurance that this downhill path is
the right one.

One hour from the top, red paint
blobs and tall white-painted CAIRNS
herald the small church of **Agios
Nikolaos** (❸; **2h**), a lovely picnic
spot. (Notice the gorgeous, isolated,
stone house across the valley!) Just
beyond the chapel your way
becomes a track. Keep straight on.
In 10 minutes pass a smallholding
on the left. Soon the landscape
opens up in front of you. Head right
at a Y-FORK (❹), on the wide track,
keeping the river bed alongside you
on the left.

Fifteen minutes later, take the
left-hand fork, staying beside the
river bed. Keep on this track for
another 20 minutes or so. At a
THREE-WAY FORK (❺) with a large
BEIGE AND YELLOW BUILDING over to
the left, take the middle prong, a
concrete path (the fork to the left
goes to the A90 highway). After
500m this path bends left, then

The sea at Kalo Horio

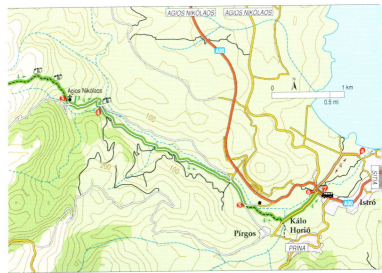

Kroustas fountain and decorated wall

right, then quickly comes to a cross-roads. Turn left; after 700m you reach the main coast road at **Istron** (**2h35min**).

Now, if you fancy a swim, turn left just *before* the main road (**6**): go under the road bridge and to the right. Walk beside the river bed,

taking the left-hand, asphalted fork. At a T-junction, turn right for the BEACH (**a**; 1km; 20 minutes). Otherwise, just turn right on the road and find the BUS STOP (**7**) on the far side, by a taverna (**2h40min**).

Walk 5: FROM KALAMAFKA TO KROUSTAS

See also photos on pages 23 (top right), 62-63 and 67
Distance: 12km/7.4mi; 3h20min
Grade: ● straightforward — along tracks most of the way; ascents/descents of 350m/1150ft overall
Equipment: walking trainers, sunhat, picnic, water
Picnic: Kefalavrisi

Access: 🚌 to Kalamafka (Males school bus; not in the timetables): departs Agios Nikolaos 06.00, 14.00 *Mon-Fri only;* journey time 40min. Or taxi if enough of you are sharing (about 25km journey). Return on 🚌 from Kroustas (not in the time-tables): buses depart 14.50 (Mon-Fri), 16.35 (Sat); no Sunday buses

This undemanding country ramble starts and ends in attractive villages and takes us through cultivated hillsides and pastures. The bus journey to Kalamafka is an experience in itself, as it's an afternoon school run and they tend to use the older buses. Take time to wander up into Kalamafka and, if you've got enough energy, look round the back streets of Kroustas, too — this is real Greece.

The bus stops in the middle of **Kalamafka** (**O**). **Start out** by walking ahead (south) through the village and take the right-hand fork when the road splits at a T-JUNCTION (**❶**), now heading north; the left fork runs south to Ierapetra). The road we are on now skirts the west side of Kalamafka. Ignore a concrete track off to the right (400m/yds from the T-junction, just before the road bends to the left). Leave the main road just after the bridge on the bend, by turning right uphill on a LANE (**❷**; **10min**). Ignore a fork to

the left after just 100m. The lane becomes a concrete track and leads to **Kefalavrisi** (❸; **15min**), the head of a spring and one of the sources of the Bramiana Reservoir circled on Walk 19 — a nice cool place for a picnic.

Cross the stream bed on the bridge shown on page 23, then stay on the track. Almost immediately, at a T-junction with a crossing track, turn left. Now on the other side of the watercourse, the track starts to climb (**30min**). When the track forks (**35min**) we usually take the route to the left, but the tracks rejoin.

Ignore two tracks going back off to the left (**1h**). The way flattens out; stay on the main route — there are VINEYARDS ahead and to the left of the track. In a couple of minutes follow the track left round the end of a vineyard. Then, after 150m, go right (❹; E4 WAYMARK on the tree here).

Soon the track starts to descend through pine trees. Turn left at a T-junction with a crossing track (**1h20min**; the E4 heads right here). In a couple of minutes (150m), when the way forks again, go right uphill. At the next fork, keep left downhill (initially on concrete). Leave the track briefly on a wide bend to the left — walking off to the right for a lovely VIEW (❺; **1h30min**) over Kalo Horio and the north coast. Rounding another bend in the track (**1h45min**), Agios Nikolaos comes into view ahead. Keep right a minute later, ignoring a track to the left.

Just after the track passes an ANIMAL SHELTER on the right (❻; **2h30min**), keep ahead, ignoring a track to the left. Then ignore the next small track downhill to the left. But just 25m further on, turn left on

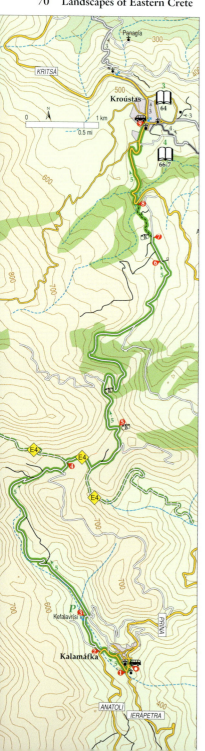

Faces of Crete

a path with FENCING on the right and a collapsed WALL on the left (**7**; **2h35min**), heading down towards the road to Prina. Just after the top of the path you have a good view of Kroustas. The stony path crosses a stretch of flatter olive groves, where the path is faint. Look for the path carrying on downhill, and *don't* be misled into striking off right on a track here.

The last section is clearly an old donkey trail, and it meets the road at a bridge. Go left over the BRIDGE (**8**; **3h10min**) and head uphill into **Kroustas**. You pass the church on your right at the start of the village. The bus from Kritsa comes in and turns round to leave where the road opens out between the houses (**9**; **3h20min**) — by the fountain shown on page 67.

Alternatively, you can walk on to Kritsa: allow about an hour and 15minutes, using the notes for WALK 3 on page 64.

Walk 6: 'BIG' SPINALONGA ISLAND

Distance: 11.3km/7mi; 2h30min
Grade: ● very easy, except for a very skiddy descent path to the beach below Agios Loukas; height difference of just over 50m/160ft. There is *no shade!*
Equipment: walking trainers, sunhat, picnic, water, swimwear
Picnic: Agios Fokas
Access: 🚌 or 🚗 to/from Elounda (Timetables 2, 7); journey time

40min. By car, park in Elounda, near the clock tower (35° 15.735'N, 25° 43.312'E) or at Olous (35° 15.447'N, 25° 44.131'E) to save 3km/2mi walking
Alternative walk: ● Adventurous walkers could use the map to cut across the island from Agios Fokas and return on an old, *overgrown* donkey trail (10.5km/6.5mi; 3h) ... *but read the introduction below!*

H aving tried to describe a pleasant, easy circuit on Spinalonga while revising the Fifth edition, Sunflower failed utterly. At the end of of a long day, we were lacerated by the *spina longa* (spiny thorns), bruised from climbing over endless drystone walls and little short of sunstruck! So unless you are an expert at cairn and waymark spotting (or you download the GPS track) stick with the main walk. It is amazingly easy to get lost on this treeless island; far better to just relax by or in the sea! And another word of caution: unless you visit out of season, be sure to walk in the morning or evening: tourist boats meet at the cove below Agios Loukas at lunchtime, with barbecues and ear-splitting music.

The walk begins at the CLOCK TOWER in **Elounda** (⭕). Follow the coastal promenade southeast round the picturesque harbour and then past the old VENETIAN SALT PANS on your right. Despite the fact that they are in ruins, if you look carefully you'll see that the various pans were separated by low stone walls — on which the workers stood to collect the evaporated salt before loading the precious cargo into the holds of Venetian trading vessels. Elounda's salt pans contributed to the wealth of Venice.
    After passing an OLD WINDMILL and crossing the small BRIDGE at **Olous** (❶; **20min**) you're on the **Spinalonga Peninsula**. (To make matters confusing, it's also called Kolokithia Island: confusing, because the small island just off its eastern shore is also called Kolokithia. And of course there are

two Spinalongas: the island we are on and the more famous one just off its north coast.) The narrow channel here — making this an island, strictly speaking, rather than a peninsula — dates from the late 1800s. It was originally dug by the Venetians, then widened by the French at the end of the 19th century, to allow ships to dock at Elounda harbour without rounding the whole peninsula. In ancient times, Olous was the site of Olounda, which gave its name to modern-day Elounda. Snorkeling in the limpid waters above the flooded ancient village is very popular.
    Just over the bridge you're greeted by the two old WINDMILLS shown overleaf, sail-less but well preserved. Motorists could park here to save 3km/40min walking. Now, before continuing, visit the 5th-century 'EARLY CHRISTIAN

BASILICA' (**2**; **25min**) with a lovely mosaic floor.

Return to the windmills, then head north on the dirt road. At a fork, go right, uphill (before the Elounda Island Villas). A paved path takes you the final steps to the little church of **Agios Loukas** (**3**; **55min**), flying the flags of Greece and the Greek Orthodox church. There's a splendid view from here down over 'little' Kolokithia — 'Bird' Island, sitting off the east coast.

Go back down the paved walkway and continue northeast on the track, then a tricky path strewn with loose stones to what the local expats call the 'HIDDEN BEACH' (**4**). But we would suggest carrying on along the good path to the restored little Byzantine church of **Agios Fokas** (**5**; **1h30min**) a bit over 1.5km to the north, where there's a walkway down to the sea for swimming — a super picnic spot (but alas, with no shade).

From there return to your car at **Olous** (**1**; **2h10min**) or, if you came by bus, vary the return by taking the track at the left of the SALT PANS to return to the CLOCK TOWER at **Elounda** (**0**; **2h30min**).

The two sail-less windmills by the parking area and basilica on Spinalonga

Walk 7: AGIOS IOANNIS POINT

We suggest three different versions of this walk; Walk c, in full sun, is best kept for cloudy, cool days.

Walk a: Aforesmenos Lighthouse (5.6km/3.5mi; 1h10min). ● Easy track walking, but can be very windy; height difference of 250m/820ft. Wear walking trainers, sunhat; take a picnic and water. Access by 🚗 along a *very eroded* concrete lane to/from Agios Ioannis church in the midst of the wind farm (35° 19.936′N, 25° 45.686′E). **Picnic** at the ruins by the church. Notes below.

Walk b: Vrouhas circuit via Agios Efraim chapel (3km/1.9mi; 1h). ● Easy; height difference of 120m/

395ft. Wear walking trainers, sunhat; take a picnic and water. Access by 🚗 to/from Vrouhas: park by the ruined mills and small church up to the right on the road from Plaka to Vrouhas (35° 18.810′N, 25° 44.158′E). **Picnic** at Agios Efraim chapel. Notes below.

Walk c: Aforesmenos Lighthouse from Plaka (17km/10.5mi; 4h). ● Only recommended for those relying on bus; fairly easy track walking, but *very long and in full sun*; height difference of 500m/1640ft; walking trainers, *sunhat*, picnic, *plenty of water*. Access by 🚌 to/from Plaka. **Picnic** as Walk a. Notes below.

Since we first walked on Agios Ioannis Point for the original edition of this guide it's been transformed by a wind farm which actually *adds* interest. It's discreet, and careful contouring ensures that it doesn't dominate everything. Whichever version of this walk you do, you'll have breathtaking views out over 'big' and 'little' Spinalonga, as well as Kolokithia — all set like precious stones in a sea which changes from pale aquamarine to deepest sapphire blue and glistens and sparkles tantalisingly all around you.

Start Walk a at the small church of **Agios Ioannis** (●), where fencing prevents vehicle access to the lighthouse. Take the path at the right of the fencing (good picnic spot), join the track and follow it down to the atmospheric old ruined **Aforesmenos Lighthouse** (❶; **30min**). *Sure-footed walkers with no fear of heights* could take the goats' path on the eastern side of the light-house to make a tiny 'circuit', but it's wiser to just retrace steps to **Agios Ioannis** (**1h10min**).

Start Walk b at the CHURCH and WINDMILLS where you park (❷): follow the main road south for 100m, then turn left on a concrete track (by several signs, including a small black and white sign indicating 'ΑΓ ΙΟΑΝΝΗΣ' and a large, colourful sign, 'ΚΑΛΩΣ ΗΛΘΑΤΕ'). After a few

minutes, leave the track and walk a short way off the route, seawards, for a wonderful views down over Spinalonga and back to Plaka — a good picnic spot.

Return to the concrete track and continue to the small, fairly new chapel of **Agios Efraim** (❸; **20min**). This is a perfect place for a picnic, with seating, stone tables — even a place to sit inside in case it rains... Climb the short lane just past the chapel, and turn left for the short stroll to Vrouhas on the smooth concrete lane, keeping left at any forks, until you come to two huge water pits (❹). If you'd like to wander around Vrouhas, you could turn right here, but we turn left, past the larger of the pits, shown overleaf, and climb up to the main road — giving the friendly local dogs

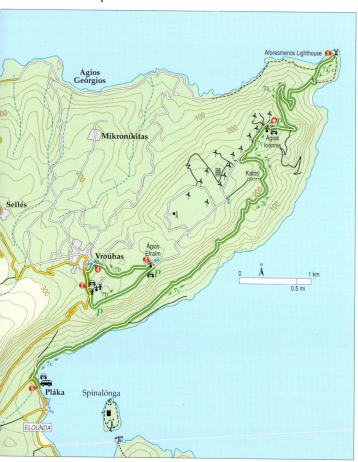

something to bark about! From here it's just a short way back to the signposted track on the left (**②**) where you parked (**1h**).

Start Walk c from the BUS STOP at **Plaka** (**⑤**): walk north along the road, with the beach on your right. When the beach ends and the road curves left, take a track off to the right. In a couple of minutes, at a Y-fork, keep right. Now simply stay on this track all the way to the CHAPEL of **Agios Ioannis** (**①**; **1h50min**), an ascent of over 250m/820ft in *full sun*.

Now follow **Walk a** to the lighthouse and back, before returning the same way to **Plaka** (**4h**)… hopefully in time for a swim in the beautiful clear water shown on page 29 before catching your bus.

Walks a and c visit the small church of Agios Ioannis shown below; Walk b calls at the chapel shown on page 74 and passes this huge water pit below Vrouhas.

Walk 8: FROM PINES TO ELOUNDA

See also photos on pages 30 and 51

Distance: 2.3km/1.4mi; 45min
Grade: ● an easy descent of 200m/650ft — a very pleasant leg-stretch when you want an undemanding day out
Equipment: walking trainers, sunhat, picnic, water, swimwear
Picnic: church above Pano Elounda

Access: 🚌 to/from Elounda (Timetables 2, 7); journey time 20min; or 🚕. To start the walk, take a taxi for the five-minute drive up to **Kato Pines**. Alight at the first building on the left after the 'Kato Pines' sign (the sign is hidden behind trees). The walk starts at the delightful buildings shown opposite.

Within minutes of leaving Elounda, you're out in the country, following in the footsteps of Cretan folk who have used these donkey trails for years. Needless to say, you will be discovering lovely views that the postcards never quite capture.

Windmill on the crest between Kato Pines and Pano Elounda

Start the walk in **Kato Pines** by taking the rising concreted alley at the right of the '*WINDMILL*' shown opposite and at the left of a small cottage with decorative latticework (**○**). After little over a minute you are at a crossroads, with one working *WINDMILL* on your left and two *SAIL-LESS MILLS* straight ahead. Go left here and walk downhill to where a donkey trail with stone walls comes in from the right (**3min**). Now follow this easy trail downhill, initially past two idyllically sited houses. You'll see several circular threshing floors like the one shown on page 51 and may be lucky enough to see people working (depending on the time of year); it's a long way from our world of combine harvesters. At the outset there are good views down over Elounda.

The road crosses your route in several minutes, but continue straight over it to rejoin the trail. Pass a small *CHURCH* on your right (a fine picnic spot, in the shade of olive trees), cross the road, and then pass another, newer *CHURCH* on the left (**❶; 14min**). Ignore the tarmac road coming in from Mavrikiano's cemetery to the left and fork right, into **Pano Elounda**. Keep straight down the narrow path ahead. Then go down wide shallow concrete steps, curving first to the left and then right. Turn left through the village, past a *cafeneion*. When you meet a crossing concrete track, follow it to the left and go under a ROAD BRIDGE (**2**; **30min**). Fork right after just 50m, cross straight over the main road

and continue down the cobbled trail, crossing another road at **Kato Elounda** (by a sign denoting the exit from **Mavrikiano**). Beyond a wide strip of tarmac/parking area, the concrete trail descends back to **Elounda** (**3**; **45min**).

To start the walk, take the walkway just at the right of the charming windmill at this flower-filled house.

See also photos pages 16, 17, 23
(bottom left) and 92-95
Distance: 14km/8.7mi; 3h55min
Grade: ● moderate, with a height
difference of 400m/1300ft; a
straightforward walk along tracks;
very little shade
Equipment: walking trainers,
sunhat, picnic, water
Picnic: just past the 30min-point
Access: 🚗 or 🚌 to the Vasiliki
turn-off (35° 4.958'N, 25° 48.844'E;
Ierapetra bus, Timetable 5; journey
time 35min). *Note:* The bus stop for

Vasiliki comes up soon after the road
turns south for Ierapetra. Look out
for a deep gorge on the left and a
sign for Monastiraki just before the
stop. (You will doubtless marvel at
the gorge; Walk 12 brings you down
here from behind it — hard to
believe?). Return on 🚌 from
Episkopi (Timetable 5; departs 10-
15 minutes after leaving Ierapetra);
journey time 10min back to the
Vasiliki turn-off to pick up your car
or 45min to Agios Nikolaos

T his moderate ramble will take you through some lovely
open countryside, with views stretching from the sea in the
north to the sea in the south, and you will have a gradual climb
over the hills facing the splendid Thripti Mountains, settings for
Walks 9, 10 and 12-15. The route takes you past Asari, an old
shepherd community, and the last section descends a wide and
easy track.

Start the walk from the BUS STOP
(⊙) by following the Vasiliki road
up to the right. Pass a sign to an
archaeological site off to the left
(**2min**). At a Y-fork as you enter
Vasiliki (❶; **15min**), keep straight
ahead (right). After curving to the
left, turn right into the main street.
Ignore the first narrow turn-off to
the left, but then take the next left
(15m/yds further on), a wider road
that leads up a slope. (There is a
triangular yellow E4 sign on a tree
opposite this road, but it's likely to
be hidden in foliage.) Along here,
take the third turn-off to the left, by
a TELEPHONE POLE (❷), just at the
top end of the village.

As it leaves Vasiliki, this track
rises, and you'll have good views of
the farmlands below, spread with a
mass of greenhouses gleaming under
the sun. In spring the hills ahead will
be covered with mauvy-pink clover
— Cretan ebony. Later in the season,

there will be bright yellow gorse
everywhere. When the many flowers
die, they are replaced by a haze of
heather, and Cretan ebony wears a
furry hat for autumn.

Ignore any turnings off this main
track for a good 800m/half a mile.
Then, at a Y-fork with a stone
building on the left, keep right
(**30min**). Ignore the turning left. In
three minutes you'll pass by a good
place for a picnic, with the lovely
view of the hills above Vasiliki
shown overleaf. Follow the E4
TRIANGLE WAYMARKS uphill, ignoring
a fork to the right. You will have a
first glimpse of the Libyan Sea off to
the left as you climb (**1h**). The track
curves right at the top of the hill and
passes under a large CAVE. From here
there are good views back down over
Vasiliki, the Dikti range, Monastiraki
and the sea off the north coast
(**1h10min**).

Following the E4 WAYMARKS,

Opposite: landscape near Vasiliki

78

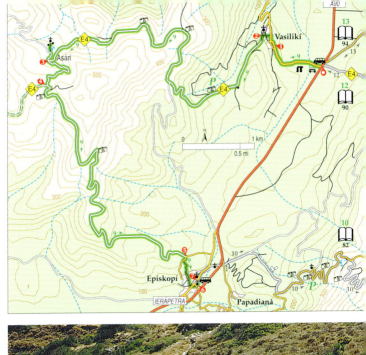

The hills above Vasiliki are pleasant for picnicking.

towards the church, passing a lovely shady place to sit, by a large water trough.

From the church return past the T-junction where you approached Asari (**❸**) and keep straight ahead, soon leaving the E4 ROUTE OFF TO THE RIGHT (**❹**; just over **2h**). Ignore the minor track off left after less than 100m. The way curves to the right and rounds a bend, giving views over the south coast. Round the next bend you'll also see Ierapetra, far off to the right: your view encompasses the south and north of the island, from the coastal flatlands around Ierapetra on your right all the way left to Kavousi (starting point for Walk 12) in the north. Straight ahead below you lies Kato Horio. The track continues downhill. There are one or two short cuts to take loops off the track but, on the whole, the old donkey trail has been destroyed.

Staying on track, you will come within sight of Episkopi and the villages opposite it (Papadiana and Ano Horio; **3h45min**). Eventually, FORK RIGHT (**❺**), then take the first left, passing a small parking area on the right. Five minutes later you will be in **Episkopi**. Head downhill until you see the main road and take the last turn-off on the left before you reach it. This will take you under the main road and round to the beautiful BYZANTINE CHURCH shown on page 16 (**❻**; **3h50min**).

Head up the slope by the church to get to the BUS STOP (**❼**; **3h55min**) and the MAIN SQUARE above it, where you can get some refreshments.

round the hill and head in a westerly direction. Keep left at a fork and, very soon, you can see Agios Nikolaos off to the right, as well as enjoying far-reaching views over the sea. The track passes a gully on the right and, three minutes later, you're off along the side of the next hill. As you round it (**1h25min**), the landscape opens out once again. A panorama of hills and slopes in varying shades of soft greens and greys spreads before you.

When the route next forks, stay left (right goes down onto a small plain where there is a triple-forked olive tree and some other trees). Before long the dilapidated couple of houses of **Asari** come into sight (**1h50min**), although the small church is intact. At a T-junction (**❷**; **1h55min**), turn right to walk

Right: climbing above the village of Episkopi on the Thripti track; it is concrete-surfaced now and was good driving before publication of the Fifth edition, but it had not yet been repaired after the 2019 storms and was very eroded when checked for this Sixth edition.

Walk 10: EPISKOPI • AGIOS IOANNIS • AGIA FOTIA

See also photo on page 16
Distance: 18km/11.2mi; 5h20min
Grade: ● fairly easy, but long; gradual, *almost shadeless* ascent to start, then descent from Agios Ioannis; almost all on tracks (the last hour is on asphalt). Height difference of 550m/1800ft
Equipment: walking trainers, sunhat, picnic, water, long trousers, swimwear
Picnic: Metamorphosis church
Access: 🚐 to Episkopi (Ierapetra bus; Timetable 5); journey time 40min. Return on 🚐 from Agia Fotia to Ierapetra (Timetables 10, 22); Sitia line departs Agia Fotia 1h after leaving Sitia; Makrigialos line departs Agia Fotia 5min after leaving Makrigialos; journey time to Ierapetra 25min. Change to 🚐 from Ierapetra to Agios

Nikolaos/Iraklion: departures almost hourly (Timetable 5); journey time 1h

Shorter walks

1   Episkopi to Agios Ioannis (9km/ 5.6mi; 2h45min). ● Grade (height difference), equipment and access as main walk. Return by 🚐 from Agios Ioannis to Agia Fotia (not in the timetables: departs 13.00 *Wednesdays only;* then bus from Agia Fotia as above). Or telephone from the *cafeneion* in Agios Ioannis for an Agia Fotia or Ierapetra taxi. Follow the main walk to Agios Ioannis.

2   Agios Ioannis to Episkopi ●
Fairly easy, with an initial ascent of 100m/330ft, then descent of 550m/ 1800ft; allow about 2h30min; access/equipment as Shorter walk 3. Use the map to reverse Shorter walk 1; route-finding is easy.

3 Agios Ioannis to Agia Fotia

(10.5km/6.5mi; 2h35min). ● Easy descent of 500m/1650ft. Equipment as main walk. 🚌 to Ierapetra (Timetable 5), then taxi or 🚌 to Agios Ioannis (not in the timetables; departs 12.15 *Wednesdays only;* journey time 45min). Return as main walk. Start at the 2h45min-point, at ❻ (page 74).

Here's a walk that leads you gently up and over the Thripti Mountains and to the south coast, where the landscape is very different from the north. Since it follows tracks or roads all the way, there is no need to watch your footing; you can stride out, enjoying the scenery. To finish, how about a swim in the Libyan Sea?

The bus stops not far past the road sign for **Episkopi** (❶), just beyond the large village church. **Start out** by walking back north along the bus route, until you reach the Agios Nikolaos end of the village. Here take the track down to the right (just by the sign showing the end of the 40km/h speed limit). After a minute you'll pass a small CHURCH (visible from the junction). Join the bypass road, cross it with care and turn left. After 30m/yds turn back sharp right into an asphalt side-road signposted to EPANO HORIO and PAPADIANA. Walk 30m/yds up this road; then, just before a POWER PYLON and WATER DISTRIBUTION POINT, turn left on a track (❶). After 50m this track forks into three. Keep to the centre track. Stay on this track until you come to a Y-fork after 350m (**15min**): go right here, heading southeast. Two minutes later (after 120m), fork right again.

You're now climbing a little, with quite gentle hillside contours creating the landscape ahead. Pass some GREENHOUSES down to the left, where there are likely to be some tied-up, barking dogs. As you reach the top of the hill, stay on the main track as it curves round to the left and descends. Meeting the THRIPTI ROAD (❷; a concrete-paved track at this point; **25min**), follow it to the left. Five minutes' climbing takes you to a very good viewpoint over the church of Papadiana, Kato Horio, and the sea beyond — a nice place to picnic. After passing the **Church of the Metamorphosis** on the left (❸; **35min**), the road curves round to the right (photo on page 83). A minute past the church there is another good picnicking spot, with glorious views all round. Soon the north coast comes into sight (**45min**).

Twenty minutes later, top up your bottle with fresh mountain water at the TROUGH on the right (**1h05min**) — you may well need it! Some 200m further on, ignore a two-wheeled track to the right. Take the *next* right turn, a rough gravel track (❹; there is a tiny, handwritten sign, 'ΣΕΛΙΜΑ' at ground level here: Selima; Thripti is indicated straight on). This turning doubles back the way you came. Now you will have a slightly steeper climb as you really get into the hills. You can still see across the island from north to

82

south. The town nestling over to your right is Vasiliki, where we start Walk 9. Ignore two minor tracks off left.

After 30 minutes' walking along this track (**1h45min**), it seems to turn back to the right. Ignore this stub of track (there is often a van parked nearby) and just keep ahead on the main route. Splendid views over towards Lasithi come up about seven minutes later, as the track winds more gently uphill. Follow the track in a U-bend to the left (**2h05min**), ignoring another stub of track straight ahead. As you round the bend you can see the top of a chapel ahead. The climb ends at the top of the hill, where **Profitis Ilias** is to your left (**5**; **2h15min**). The chapel is usually open, and the views — this time over the south and east — are splendid.

A couple of minutes from the chapel, at a fork, keep to the lower track. When the track splits again after 100m, turn right in a tight hairpin bend. At the next fork, 150m further on, curl down to the left. Soon you cross over what was once a mountain river and is now completely dry. Rock rises high above you, and oleander bushes flourish to your right, their bright pink flowers creating a vibrant contrast to the browns of the landscape. Coming into **Agios Ioannis** (**6**; **2h45min**), you'll find a welcome *cafeneion*. It's possible to call a taxi from here if you want a quick route to the sea!

To make for Agia Fotia, leave Agios Ioannis on the road signposted '*AGII SARANDA*'. After a few bends the road curves round to the right, and a church that looks as if it has been built of crazy paving, with red domes, comes into view

Leaving Agios Ioannis, a church that looks as if it has been built of crazy paving comes into view down to the right.

down to the right. But we walk away from this CEMETERY CHURCH, taking a left turn onto a concreted track. Not far along, we round the fertile valley leading from Agios Ioannis to the sea. (At the head of this valley, ignore a faint track off left.) On the descent you will enjoy some good views back up to Agios Ioannis. As the main village disappears from sight (**3h05min**), stay on the right-hand, lower track.

Some 200m further on, ignore a track heading sharply back to the right. After another 120m, take the higher, left-hand track — starting to curl left to almost encircle a SOLAR PANEL 'FARM' up to the left. As you round this bend, the scene changes from one of green cultivation to open landscape. An enormous mountain spreads before you, with a transmitter and tiny church as a centrepiece — Stavromenos, the goal of Walk 14. It is useful to *keep this church in mind* as a landmark, as there are many new tracks criss-crossing the way, going to various olive groves and smallholdings.

After about 10 minutes (from turning the bend), you'll see another track going up to the left — ignore it, and stay on the main route here. After another five minutes, ignore another track going off left and keep on the main track. In another five minutes, stay on the main (lower) track to the right. Immediately after crossing a small stream, this track forks. The right-hand fork is your ongoing route, but first take the left-hand fork to make a short detour to a pleasant resting spot next to the church of **Agia Paraskevi** (❼), surrounded by tall cool pines and olive groves, beside a gushing stream. Then retrace your steps from this cul-de-sac and take the other fork.

This track is concreted for several metres, then peters out into a faint track or path. It leads across an olive grove and another stream set in a gully. About 120m after crossing the stream, be sure to head up left at a fork, to rise up onto a track to continue. Turn right on this track and follow it for 20 minutes, then head right at a Y-fork. This track eventually curves round from the sea and meets an ASPHALT ROAD two minutes later (❽; **4h20min**): turn right. You will be on asphalt now for almost an hour, until you come to the main road at the end of the walk. A few minutes along, at a THREE-WAY FORK, keep right.

About half an hour later you will see plastic greenhouses down in the valley to the left (**4h55min**). Now there is only 25 minutes between you and the lovely sparkling sea at Agia Fotia beach. What about a hang glider?

The road now turns away from the sea and back towards the mountains, giving you a chance to look out over the hills you've just crossed. Curve round the greenhouses and soon come to the MAIN SOUTH COAST ROAD. Turn right for 50m, to a BUS SHELTER (❾; **5h20min**). Remember to catch your bus on the inland side of the road for your journey to Ierapetra.

Walk 11: FROM SFAKA TO TOURLOTI

See also photos on pages 14-15, 54
Distance: 13km/8mi; 3h30min
Grade: ●: moderate; a gradual (long) ascent to begin; height difference of 530m/1740ft; possibility of vertigo
Equipment: walking trainers, sunhat, water (none en route), picnic
Picnic: 12min-point or after

Access: 🚌 to Sfaka (Sitia bus, Timetables 6, 8; journey time 1 hour). Or 🚗 to Sfaka (35° 9.278'N, 25° 55.401'E). Return on 🚌 from Tourloti (Sitia bus, Timetables 6, 8) — back to your car at Sfaka or back to base. Departs Tourloti 30min after leaving Sitia; journey time to Agios Nikolaos 1h05min.

Here's a pleasant loop for keen walkers that leads you through hillside pastureland and the heart of a farming community. Open countryside fringes the mountains, and you're never far from the sight of the sea.

As you approach the village of **Sfaka** (●), the bus stops by the POST OFFICE on the right, where a side road leads off uphill. **Start out** by walking back west towards Agios Nikolaos on the main road. After just a few paces, turn right up shallow steps with railings alongside them (just behind road signs for Sitia and Agios Nikolaos). At the top, turn right on a road which heads through the village houses up towards the mountain behind them. Soon the road becomes a motor track (**5min**). Start curving round to the right on this track, then take the donkey path that goes off to the left (just over 100m/yds after the track is concreted for a short way). Soon you'll have a nice view back over Sfaka and its church. Rejoining the main track (**12min**), you can look out straight over Sfaka all the way to Tourloti, your destination — your way is over the mountains ahead. Set just off the road, a little way past Tourloti, is Mirsini — the next coastal village on the road to Sitia.

As you rejoin the track at this good lookout point (from here on, anywhere is pleasant for picnicking), ignore the inviting looking track opposite — unless you want to picnic in someone's garden! Turn left and follow the track round a couple of bends (ignoring a left turn signposted to ПРОФ.НΛΙΑ on the first bend). After the second bend you'll be looking straight across to Askordalia (1238m/4060ft), the highest peak in the Orno range. The coastline is fast receding, but the ascent is quite gradual. The track crosses a dried-up stream which the local people may still be using as a RUBBISH TIP (**18min**). Curve around and, within a minute (100m after another concreted section ends), just where you can see the main road below you, strike off left up another small donkey path that may well be somewhat overgrown. As it forms a 'T', go left; then walk on and head towards the stone wall above. The path turns into rubble and widens out. You can see the bends of the main track below you — proving that you're shortening your walk. When the path rejoins the track, turn left. You can see Lastros now with its church in the foreground. After about 10-12 minutes, on a hairpin bend to the right (and with a couple of buildings to the left, at the edge of terracing), go left on a minor track cutting through vineyards. Walk to the left of a shed, meet a minor track and turn right. You join the main track again after 70m: turn left.

From here it's easy to make out

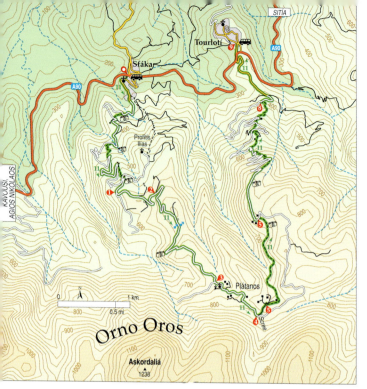

the half-hidden Psira ('Flea') Island
and the small dot of an island called
Agios Nikolaos, both just off the
coast at Mohlos. When the track
next forks (**❶**; **1h**), keep left uphill.
You see the isolated church of
Profitis Ilias again, which you may
have first noticed as you climbed up
through the village at the start of the
walk. Soon pass some DWELLINGS
and ANIMAL SHELTERS off to the left,
but don't take the track down to
them. You've been able to enjoy level
walking for some time now, but
soon the way starts to climb again
(gradually), after you pass by a
WINNOWING AND THRESHING CIRCLE
on your right (**1h05min**). The
isolated church is now just between
you and Sfaka. When the track forks
on a concreted section (**❷**;
1h10min), keep right, to the upper
way. Then stay on this track as it
makes a hairpin bend to the right.

Ten minutes later, come to a
T-junction with a tree at the right.
Turn right and head towards the
mountains. Soon you pass another
WINNOWING AND THRESHING CIRCLE
on the left and then deep STONE
WELLS (similar in construction to
Minoan wells) either side and go
through two DOUBLE METAL GATES
(**1h25min**). Five minutes later,
rounding a hairpin bend to the left,
you'll have a good view of a gorge
below to the right, as it heads down
to the sea. Then you'll lose sight of
the sea altogether. Soon spot another
collection of stone buildings up to
the right.

Another church comes into sight.
A few minutes later, you pass
through another pair of METAL
GATES. Then the track divides again
(**❸**; **1h43min**). Take the left-hand
fork, towards the church. Before
long, having passed the CHURCH,
you'll approach a group of dwellings
on a stony outcrop. This is **Platanos**

(**1h45min**), the heart of the farming and shepherd community enlivening this landscape. Their livelihood is spread out all around you — fruit trees, almond and walnut trees, vines, figs and pastureland. Massive, rounded mountains encircle you. As you walk towards a STONE WALL AND A SHELTER, the track bends round to the right. Follow it round, then bend left again. If you look over to the left, you'll see the line of the path you'll follow up to a pass before you descend to Tourloti; it cuts out a large swathe of track.

Soon the track abuts a line of SCREE (**1h50min**). Just before here, turn left on the track that heads towards some houses (**❹**; **1h50min**). You'll be walking seawards again, although the sea is not yet in sight. Some 250m/yds down the track you may have to undo a pair of GATES if there is no one working nearby who has left them open. Past the gates there's a house to the right with pretty wrought iron gates. Take the track/wide path just to the right of the drive to the house (**❺**). Then undo another gate in another wire fence just at the left of a RUSTED WATER TANK, beyond which is your path up the hill to the pass.

Suddenly, through a V in the mountains ahead, you see the coast and the glistening blue sea (**2h**). The 'dinosaur's back' of rock on the far side of the tree-lined river bed arches towards the sea now, just as the trail narrows. This path turns away from the river bed, to the right. Some people may find this path a bit unnerving, especially if they are prone to vertigo, because it is so high. However, the drops are not sheer, and the walking is easy and level.

Buildings come into sight up ahead on the left, at the end of the

path and, if you look towards the sea, you'll see the granite quarry scar above Mohlos again and little Psira Island, still slightly hidden behind the coast. Once you reach here, away from the edge of the river bed gorge, the possibility of vertigo is lessened. And then you're back on a track again (**❻**; **2h20min**; there's more wire netting just before the path meets the track). Join the track and turn left, passing the buildings. In ten minutes, this track runs between a stone wall and a fence. From here there are lovely views of your destination, Tourloti, the north coast, Sfaka to your left, and Mirsini to the right. This is a nice place to take a break before descending for the last part of the walk.

As the track begins to descend now and makes its first loop, you'll see a SHORT-CUT PATH (**❼**) going off straight ahead. Follow it until it joins the track again. Continue down to the right on the track until, at the next bend, you can again use the path as a short cut. When the path splits, take the lower fork, to the right. When you next meet the track, step down over rocks, walk right, round the next bend and take a path off to the right. Watch your footing on the loose stones. Join the track again and follow it to the right of vineyard terracing. Soon (**2h50min**) you'll be taking another short-cut path. This one is angled back from the track. It starts out just beyond a slab-like piece of flat rock. The path becomes overgrown and goes through knee-high undergrowth. It skirts round vine-growing plots and passes behind a stone building. The path widens out beyond the building. Look for the path going left, towards Tourloti. Continue on it, and soon you will meet another track. Turn left and continue on down; within metres, where the

main track crosses, turn right. Then, as a track forks back to the left, continue on for a few metres and take the path going off left. This path gets wider as we near the outskirts of Tourloti. Rejoining the track, turn left, then take the path off right again. Then join the track once more and follow it to the right downhill. You'll pass a STONE BUILDING WITH A COWLED METAL CHIMNEY, as the track bends left. A minute or so past here, take the minor track curving back off to the right. Within a very short distance, it appears to end. Walk down to the

right, onto a path (there's a wall on the right of this path). Curve round a DERELICT BUILDING on the left. Meet the MAIN TRACK again (**8**; **3h15min**) and turn right; there's a large fig tree on your right.

Follow the track, then road, round a bend to the left and walk on towards the village and find the main road just ahead below you. A sign points you towards **Tourloti**. As the BUS STOP (**9**; **3h30min**) is in the village, why not aim for the centre right now and have a well-earned rest and refreshing drink?

Springtime at Platanos

See also photos on pages 14-15, 17, 23 (bottom left), 94-95, 99
Distance: 15.9km/9.9mi; 6h
Grade: ● for the energetic. This walk involves a strenuous climb lasting 2h; you must be sure-footed, too, for the last half hour of descent. Height difference of 800m/2625ft. Almost all E4
Equipment: walking trainers or boots, long trousers, sunhat, picnic, plenty water and fruit
Picnic: 15-30min above Kavousi

Access: 🚐 to Kavousi (Sitia bus, Timetables 6, 8); journey time 40min. Return on 🚐 from the Monastiraki turn-off (Ierapetra bus, Timetable 5). Departs 10-15 minutes after leaving Ierapetra; journey time 35min
Short walk: Thripti to Monastiraki (9km/5.6mi; 3h). ● Moderate descent (about 800m), but you must be sure-footed; almost all E4. By taxi or with friends to Thripti (❹) and follow the walk from there.

W e have tried not to put too many 'dos' and 'don'ts' in our book; however, some walks — like this one — demand it ... if only to heighten your sheer enjoyment of it all! This is one of the walks that starts out in the east of the island, so we urge you to catch the early bus. The sunrise, particularly at the beginning and the end of summer, is simply magnificent. Also, before you embark on this walk, do take one of the nearby walks — Walk 9, 10 or 13. From one of these you will see the splendid, dramatic cleft of the Ha Gorge at Monastiraki. At the end of this walk, you'll have the wonderful satisfaction of having walked high up behind this gorge.

This walk requires stamina, but the rewards are great, and you'll feel tremendously exhilarated — at one with the landscape — as you climb higher and higher into those splendid mountains, spellbound by the views. You can anticipate a friendly welcome in Thripti and a pleasant contrast of scenery from village to hillside — via vineyards, pasturelands and mountains, where the local people scratch a living high in the hills.

Start out at the BUS STOP in **Kavousi** (**O**), an attractive village on the main coast road. Set off by following the main road downhill towards the large white CHURCH shown overleaf. But after just a few paces, turn left up a lane with a GREEN E4 SIGN for 'THRIPTI' (on the wall behind you). Walk past a supermarket on the left and a SCHOOL PLAYGROUND on the right. After under 200m/yds you come to the VILLAGE SQUARE, at the far end of which you'll see a building with five steps leading up to it. Turn left in

front of it, and keep left and uphill, leaving the village; you pass to the left of **Agios Georgios Church** (**❶**). The concrete will become a rough path and then a more obvious donkey trail. This route is part of the E4 trail, so keep an eye out for the YELLOW PAINT WAYMARKS.

Just past a RED-DOMED CHURCH, you pass a concrete and dirt road off left (**8min**). Three minutes later, pass a square WATER TANK on the left and cross another dirt road — going straight over. Keep beside the CONCRETE WATERCOURSE,

89

occasionally pushing past overhanging carob trees. The path opens out and you arrive back on the road, here concreted. Follow it to the left for about 170m, then fork left on a farm track. After only 30m turn right up the cobbled donkey trail marked with some YELLOW WAYMARKS AND SMALL CAIRNS. If the climbing doesn't take your breath away, the views will! You can now see all the way from Agios Nikolaos to the tip of Agios Ioannis Point beyond Plaka — a pleasant area for picnicking.

When you meet the concreted road again, turn left for about 100m, to see the ISLAND'S OLDEST OLIVE TREE (photo on page 99; **25min**) — perhaps the oldest *Olea europea* in Europe. A sign nearby tells you that it's some 14m high (over 46 feet); its diameter at the base of the trunk is just under 5m (over 16ft) and the circumference 22m (over 72ft). It would appear, from ring dating, to be 3250 years old. The island classes some of its olive trees as 'monu-mental', and this is the grand-daddy of them all, planted in early Minoan times.

From the tree turn back along the road to where you came up and head left to continue up the trail (YELLOW WAYMARK on the ground on the left). Look for the waymarks; the path can be quite overgrown, depending on the time of year. When you can see an OLD HOUSE ahead (just under **1h**), follow the path as it curves left uphill — don't go straight ahead across the hillside towards the building. You should pass to the right of a RUINED CHURCH and then a SPRING (❷) in a stand of oaks.

In another 10 minutes, we will have led you up to a height of

500m/1650ft (**1h10min**). If you are inclined to suffer from vertigo, don't peer over into the gorge. Kavousi lies in an impressive spread below you now. The path comes up to a level, more open area: turn left here on a good donkey trail (**1h15min**). By this time the gradient is 1 in 3 — hard work! You will realise how aerobic walking can be as you approach the top. Ten minutes later (**1h25min**) the trail forks: keep *right and uphill*, to continue towards Thripti. (Continuing to the left would take you to Kastro; see Walk 15.)

On reaching a PASS at the top of the trail (825m; **1h55min**), take the wide dirt road in front of you, keeping the deep valley with its zigzag tracks off to your left. You will follow this road for the next half hour or so. It meanders pleasantly through an abundance of wild flowers — if it's the right time of year — and you should be able to spot some pretty pink orchids amongst them.

The scenery at the top of the climb changes: it's green and hilly, with a sprinkling of vineyard terracing. Looking behind you, the large awesome mountain overlooking this landscape is Kliros. To the west of it is the hamlet of Drakalevri. More buildings soon come into sight, heralding the beginnings of Thripti. Ignore a minor track off left to houses, then fork right, by one or two houses on the right (❸; **2h30min**). *(Walk 15a turns left here, to make for Tsamantis.)* Some 150m further on, keep straight on at a THREE-WAY FORK — where the concrete road you are on makes a U-bend to the left. Three minutes later, at a T-junction, turn left, past more old buildings. It's surprising how

Left: Kavousi church, where the walk begins

The walk comes into Monastiraki at the taverna shown above and on page 23, then you join Walk 13 at waypoint 8. The photo below of the gorge was taken on Walk 13.

such seemingly unproductive land can be cultivated, and more than likely, you'll see people busily tending their vines around you, or even picking grapes — if it's early October. Look beyond the church rising up in the middle of Thripti, and you'll see the coast and sea beyond … a long way away.

At the next junction (a Y-fork), turn right and keep on this main street through **Thripti** (❹; **2h40min**), ignoring any streets to the right (the first of which heads back uphill to the church). Some 400m from the Y-fork, just beyond a TAVERNA on the right, you come to the far side of the village, where the narrow road to the right comes up from Kato Horio and the concreted track to the left heads off towards Stavromenos (Walk 14). This triangular, crazy-paved 'SQUARE' (**2h50min**) boasts two FOUNTAINS (to your left). But if you are after something a bit more sustaining than water, it's worth stopping at the taverna, which will doubtless welcome your custom if it's open — a good chance to practise some Greek phrases.

With your back to the fountains, walk away from Thripti on the Kato Horio road. Within a few minutes, at a break in the ROADSIDE BARRIER (**5**), take a track leading down to the right —despite the lack of E4 signposting. Keep straight on, ignoring a first turning to the right after four-five minutes and another after 15 minutes (*but note that the E4 takes this second turning to the right*). We keep to the main track: before long you will be walking through pine trees — where you may see some beehives. Five minutes further on, keep down right; then, half a minute later, keep down right again. At the next fork keep straight on. Follow the track as it bends right, then fork right, downhill once more — heading towards the gorge. (*Note that the E4 does not fork right here, but keeps left on the major track. They rejoin shortly; we prefer this lower track.*)

Some 55 minutes from leaving Thripti (**3h50min**) there is a tremendous view straight through the top of Ha Gorge and over to the village of Vasiliki (Walk 9). Two minutes later (about an hour from Thripti) the track rises to another track coming up from the Kato Horio road. Now back on the E4 route, follow this track to the right, and half a minute later you will come to the church of **Agia Anna** (**6**), where the track forks. Keep right, downhill. At the next fork keep down right again.

Rounding the top of **Ha Gorge** (1h15min from Thripti; **4h10min**) you'll enjoy a fabulous view over Pahia Ammos and the bay. Keep on the lower track (1h20min from Thripti) and five minutes later you will reach the lowest point in the track, where there is a stream bed and some oleanders. Cross the stream bed and turn right on a track.

On the first big bend to the left, strike off right on an old path (**7**; 1h25min from Thripti; **4h20min**), which heads downhill to the left. Soon you may be picking your way through pine trees and over fallen ones.

Soon (1h35min from Thripti; **4h30min**) you can feast your eyes on another fantastic panorama. You're now high above the main road, with views of Ierapetra, the setting for Walk 10, and all the way round north to Agios Nikolaos. From this marvellous lookout point you also have a perfect view over Vasiliki and the hills of Walk 9, shown on pages 79 and 80. Beyond them, to the west, lie the hills of Lasithi (Walks 22-25). On more than one occasion, we have stood here transfixed, marvelling at the changing colours, patterns and textures of this wonderful landscape. You are heading south now. Some 2h05min from Thripti (**5h**), at a junction with a large spread of oleander, waymarking directs you in a southerly direction. (There is also waymarking heading north, downhill, back the way you came.) Eighteen minutes later the path joins a track. Turn right to continue. The track leads you into pretty **Monastiraki** (**8**). Arriving in the village, walk down steps, past the well-sited TAVERNA shown opposite and CHURCH. Turn left at the bottom of the steps and wend your way through some dilapidated old houses.

Emerging on the far side, fork right on a track and head towards the main road. After 100m take a small track leading off right. This track (still the E4) leads to the main road. The BUS STOP is on the left (**9**; 3h05min from Thripti; **6h**).

Walk 13: HA GORGE

See also photos on pages 17, 23, 92, 94, 95 and the cover
Distance: 4.5km/2.8mi; 1h20min
Grade: ● very easy except for the short but awkward crossing of the

gorge mouth; height difference of 120m/390ft
Equipment: trainers, long trousers, sunhat, picnic, water
Picnic: Ha Gorge
Access: ⛟ to/from Monastiraki: park at the first asphalted turn-off right (35° 5.365'N, 25° 49.408'E) or 🚐 to/from the village turn-off (Ierapetra bus, Timetable 5; departs 10 minutes after leaving Ierapetra; journey time 35min)
Short walk: Ha Gorge (30min; ● easy). Park at the paper mill; walk to the mouth of the gorge (by the info board shown opposite) and back.

Without being proficient at canyonning or fit enough for Walk 12, it is still possible to get up close to the awesome Ha Canyon on this walk which is suitable for all-comers. We would only suggest that if you plan to take pictures, do the walk late in the afternoon for the best light.

Park at the first asphalted turn-off right (○), 1km along the road into Monastiraki (bus users coming from the main road should allow an extra 10-15 minutes to this point). Continue along this road, passing an atmospheric derelict FACTORY and a car inspection garage. Turn right at the next asphalted junction and walk past a thriving PAPER MILL, towards a CHAPEL ahead. Then just keep on the track: INFORMATION PANELS at the end of the track mark the MOUTH OF THE GORGE (❶; 30min). Just ahead you'll see a path on the far side of the river bed, and although it's a very short way, you may need to negotiate the awkward crossing by backside — the soil is littered with loose stones.

While the only spectacular part of this walk is the gorge itself, there is much else to delight and amuse — from the tiny white chapel against its awesome backdrop to the yappy lapdog 'guard' behind the paper mill fence and the circuitry of water distribution points.

The path on the far side is much prettier, weaving its way amid greenery and oleander, with pale blue dots to guide you. Meeting a track, follow it into the upper part of **Monastiraki**, then go right, down STEPS (❷; **55min**), past the TAVERNA and CAR PARK. This part of the village has been rebuilt with EU funds, and very pretty it is too. Now either walk ahead to your car (❍) or go left for the BUS (❸; **1h20min**).

This walk explores the mouth of the gorge, shown here on the approach, with an info board neaarby. The gorge is a popular canyonning venue...

Walk 14: STAVROMENOS

See also photo on page 6
Distance: 7km/4.3mi; 3h30min
Grade: ●: a long, steep climb and descent of 630m/2066ft; you must be sure-footed, with a head for heights; faint waymarks
Equipment: walking trainers or boots, sunhat, picnic, plenty of drinking water and fruit, long trousers
Picnic: in the pines (after 35min)

Access: 🚗 only accessible by car to Thripti (via a narrow road rising from Kato Horio). Leave your car at the edge of the village, at a crazy-paved 'square' (35° 5.341'N, 25° 51.694'E). Or, if you're really fit and enjoy long-distance walking, follow Walk 12 to Thripti and continue up to Stavromenos before heading for Monastiraki.

Getting to Thripti is a bit of an adventure in itself, in that you follow a narrow, high-mountain road for 7km of the 11km drive from Kato Horio. And the ascent of Stavromenos is challenging, taking you from a mountain community to above the clouds. From the top you can see far out over the south and north coasts of the island and really feel a sense of achievement.

Facing the FOUNTAINS in the slab-paved 'SQUARE' (**O**) at the edge of **Thripti**, **start out** by taking the concreted track to the right. (The village street straight ahead, marked with a 'no entry' sign, passes a taverna and is where Walk 12 comes into Thripti.) Just under 400m/yds along this track (**5min**), turn sharp right uphill on another concreted track. Ignore turnings right (after 50m) and left (100m further on) to houses. After another 50m follow the main track in a U-bend to the right (**15min**). Then, almost at once, turn up 90° left (waymarked), then 90° right. The track becomes a rough path — going via some WAYMARKED BUILDINGS — for about 50m. When you meet a crossing track, where there is a TAP opposite, go straight over and continue up a path. This path widens to track again. Leave it after 70m by turning right (**20min**), either on a waymarked path or up a flight of steps next to it, by a sign in Greek, 'ΟΔΟΣ ΞΠΨΣΑΓΓΕΛΟΝ'.

Continue on up, passing fields of vines and WAYMARKED, DESERTED BUILDINGS. The path comes up onto a GRAVEL TRACK (**27min**); you are already high over Thripti by now. Turn right and after 100m turn sharp left uphill on another track. You may have to pass through a fence on the ascent; there is a GATE. Six minutes from joining this track, at a THREE-WAY FORK (**❶**; **35min**),

turn right into pine trees (a CAIRN and WAYMARKING indicate the route). Follow the waymarks and CAIRNS carefully here (not always obvious if they're hidden by the pine needles underfoot) and continue upwards, eventually moving out of the pine trees (**45min**) and then on through another, smaller band of pines. Then the path becomes rough, grey stones as you climb higher and higher up almost bare mountainside.

Soon, on a small COL (**1h**) there's a chance to catch your breath. After 20 more minutes of climbing, the terrain levels out on a PLATEAU (**1h20min**) ... but you are not quite at your destination! A large transmitter is up ahead, and you can see your onward track carved into the hillside ahead, leading to it. Beyond, up to the right of the transmitter, is the small chapel at the end of the ascent.

Eventually the waymarked path meets the TRACK (❷; **1h30min**) that loops ahead uphill. Join the it and

turn right, continuing the ascent. In another 20 minutes, having left the TRANSMITTER off to the left, you reach the viewing terrace and the CHAPEL of **Afendis Christos** at the SUMMIT of **Stavromenos** (❸; **2h**). The door needs a good push!

After enjoying the dramatic view over the north and south coasts — and doubtless picnicked — turn round and head back to **Thripti** (❍; **3h30min**) for some *real* sustenance — like *raki*.

Walk 15: MESONAS GORGE

See also photos on pages 14-15, 54 and 90
Note: We suggest three different versions of this walk, but all have the following in common:
Access: 🚌 to/from Kavousi (Sitia bus, Timetables 6, 8; journey time 40min); or 🚗 to Kavousi: use the car park off the E4 Thripti walking route (35° 7.356'N, 25° 51.508'E)
Equipment: walking boots, sunhat, water, picnic
Picnic: in the gorge
Grade: ●: In addition to the grade for individual suggestions, *all* versions are fairly strenuous, with an initial climb of over 2h, and all
versions follow an exposed water channel through a gorge. Although there are railings at most exposed points, you must be sure-footed and have a head for heights.
Walk a: Mesonas Gorge via the Thripti ascent approach (14km/8.7mi; 5h50min); height difference of 750m/2460ft. See text below.
Walk b: Mesonas Gorge via the motor track approach (13.5km/8.4mi; under 5h); height difference of 630m/2070ft. See text below.
Walk c: Ascent of the Mesonas Gorge (*up to* 14km/8.7mi; 5-6h); height difference of *up to* 750m/2460ft. See text below.

There are *so* many ways to tackle this hike and *so much* to see — from a bubbling watercourse to what may be Europe's oldest olive tree, from the Thripti mountains to a clutch of ancient Minoan sites. But we'd recommend Walk c to anyone who is unsure of their reaction to steep unprotected drops. Walk *up* the gorge, and if you're out of your comfort zone, go back. The most difficult stretch, shown overleaf, is not far below the ruined hamlet of Tsamantis, at the top.

Start Walk a in Kavousi (●) by following Walk 12 to the FORK at the **2h30min**-point. Turn left here, and follow this track, via **Drakalevri**, for just under 4km/2.5mi, until you come to a wide path off left leading to the ruins of the old hamlet of **Tsamantis** (❹; **3h30min**). Now pick up WALK B AT THE 2H30MIN-POINT, and add about 1h to all cumulative times.

Start Walk b at the BUS STOP near the CHURCH on the main road in **Kavousi** (●): walk east for a couple of minutes, towards Sitia, then turn right at a BROWN SIGN FOR VARIOUS ARCHAEOLOGICAL SITES — among them Azoria, Kastro and Vronda, all of which you could visit on this walk. The narrow road makes straight for the **Thripti mountains** and the gorge we'll descend later in the walk. After just 100m/yds, turn left on a farm track through an olive

grove. On the far side, just before the entrance to a gorge, turn left on an old DONKEY TRAIL (❶). This ancient trail climbs the left flank of the ever-steepening **Havgas Gorge** below the summit of **Kliros** in the **Orno range**. Almost straight away there are breathtaking views to the Gulf of Mirabello and Agios Nikolaos in the distance — as well as into the depths of this gorge.

The trail eventually emerges on the motor track to Tsamantis (and Thripti; ❷; **40min**): keep straight ahead here, uphill. You can already look up to see the the line of the concrete water channel at the edge of the **Mesonas Gorge**. Ignore the path down to a chapel on the right and carry on to the first houses of **Melisses**, a hamlet of buildings scattered between small fields, olive groves and fig trees (**1h05min**). By the first building, head right at a fork

signed to 'THRIPTI', immediately
crossing a stream. Then continue
along this main dirt road. After
about 10 minutes, you pass two
gated tracks off left (only about
100m apart). After another 15
minutes or less, at a fork, bear right.
The road climbs in hairpins to a PASS
(**❸**) at 710m/2330ft: once over the
pass, you have a fine view to
Stavromenos with its transmitter
tower and chapel (Walk 14).

Twenty minutes later the road
crosses a stream bed and then, after
only 150 metres, a WATER CHANNEL
set into the road. Here follow
YELLOW WAYMARKS leading you
down to the abandoned hamlet of
Tsamantis (**❹**; **2h30min**), its stone
houses overgrown with oaks,
almond and fig trees — an exquisite
and romantic setting, perfect for a
picnic.

Follow the water channel half
right down to the houses, from
where the channel — cradling a fat
water pipe — crosses to the other
side of the valley. Now walk along
the maintenance path beside the
channel. About 15-20 minutes from
Tsamantis the valley narrows to
become the wild upper **Mesonas**

Signpost at the lower end of the gorge;
Kavoúsi's monumental olive tree; Kliros is
the mountain overlooking these walks

Gorge, with vertiginous drops to the depths below. This is a *very exposed part of the walk*; soon the channel crosses to the other side of the gorge via an aqueduct with protective railings.

And all of a sudden the channel is filled with sparkling rushing water! At a point where the watercourse turns 90° to the left, you can turn right to a brilliant *VIEWPOINT* (**5**; **3h15min**) over the Mirabello Gulf — and the wind farm on Agios Ioannis Point (Walk 7). Not far beyond the viewpoint is a another particularly vertiginous stretch of path, where you have to edge protruding rock.

Some 20 minutes past the viewpoint the water channel heads left, away from the gorge. About 250m further on, watch for a *YELLOW WAYMARK* signalling a path half-right. Follow this short but skiddy path down to a farm track and follow this straight ahead (right). After just 60m you meet the motorable track to Melisses and Tsamantis at the signposts shown on page 99 — just opposite the Minoan settlement of **Azoria** (**6**). Take the path between stone walls up to the site (**3h55min**), from where there's a wonderful view down to Kavousi. This sizeable, fascinating settlement was destroyed by a fire and is still being excavated by volunteers — you can have an interesting chat with them if they're working.

Then return to the dirt road and turn right through olive groves and cypresses. Beyond an olive grove you come to a small *CHAPEL* and then the famous 3250-year-old *MONUMENTAL OLIVE TREE* shown on page 99 (**7**; Walk 15a has already been here on

the ascent and can simply retrace steps to Kavousi). Keep to the dirt road for another 100m, then turn right down a cobbled donkey trail (*YELLOW WAYMARK*). When this meets another dirt road, turn right downhill. A *YELLOW WAYMARK* signals where you rejoin the trail off to the right. The trail crosses the road once more, then descends to the outskirts of **Kavousi** (**4h50min**), from where you can follow your nose to the main road and *BUS STOP* (●).

Start Walk c in Kavousi (●) by using the notes for Walk 12 to the *MONUMENTAL OLIVE TREE* at the **25min**-point. Continue on the dirt road from here, passing a chapel (**35min**). Keep to the road; opposite the path to the **Azoria** *SITE* (**6**), the signpost shown on page 99 alerts you to a farm track running half-right up the hillside. Follow this, then, when the track makes a hairpin bend to the right, go straight ahead up a loose-stone path to a *WATER CHANNEL* (there should be a yellow dot waymark here). Now just follow this up the lower, then the upper **Mesonas Gorge** for as long as you feel comfortable.

If you make it all the way to **Tsamantis** (**4**), you will have a choice of return routes: retrace your steps (noting that it is often more difficult *descending* than ascending vertiginous paths), descend the dirt road via Melisses, walk on towards Thripti and descend the Walk a ascent route (E4 *WAYMARKED*), or follow the tracks and paths shown on the map to visit two other Minoan sites: Kastro and Vronda — although there is less to see than at Azoria.

Left: The top photo shows the most difficult part of the walk, where the water pipe drops into the gorge and is carried to the other side in an aqueduct. You won't have to slither down beside the pipe or cross the aqueduct, but you will have to descend the very steep path at the right of the pipe, just below the walker. At the bottom of the photo a handrail is visible at the right of the path. Stow all gear before this descent! The walk then continues on the metal plates (also with handrail), after which the water flows freely in its channel and you descend gently to Kavousi and the sea.

Walk 16: RICHTIS GORGE

Distance: 10km/6.2mi; 3h45min (4h15min for bus users who alight at the Exo Mouliana bus stop)

Grade: ● sometimes challenging gorge walk, with a height difference of 430m/1410ft; you must be sure-footed and agile

Equipment: walking trainers, sunhat, long trousers, water, picnic, bathing things

Picnic: in the gorge or at the tree-shaded tables at the beach

Access: 🚗 or 🚌 to/from Exo Mouliana (Sitia bus, Timetables 6, 8; journey time 1h30min). By car or on foot, from the bus stop go 450m south to the sign 'GORGE OF RICHTIS', where there is a car park on the main road (35° 9.853'N, 25° 59.343'E).

Short walk: Richtis Beach to the waterfall (3.2km/2mi; 1h15min). ● Easy; equipment as above. 🚗 to/from Richtis Beach (35° 11.770'N, 25° 59.059'E): the road, signed 'BEACH OF RICHTIS', is just west of the bus shelter in Exo Mouliana. *Warning: This very narrow road, with precipitous, unprotected drops, is only suitable for confident drivers and passengers.* The road ends at a sign for the gorge, but turn left on a track to the beach and park in the shade of tamarisk trees (**4**). Walk back to the sign for the gorge and follow it to the WATERFALL (**3**), then return.

The jungle-like Richtis Gorge is one of the most exhilarating experiences you can enjoy in Eastern Crete. Its reputation is spreading so quickly that we fear it will become the Samaria of the east: if at all possible, walk here out of the 'season' or very early in the day.

Start out by following the lane (later track) from the 'GORGE OF RICHTIS' car park on the main road to **Lachanas Bridge** (**1**). Then head north under the bridge on a cart track. There are handwritten signs and variously coloured waymarks to guide you. The first kilometre or so is quite easy, in deep shade alongside the stream, and brings you to a ruined MILL (**2**) where olives were crushed.

Beyond the overgrown mill the going gets trickier: the descent is steep at times, and you'll be clambering over smooth, slippery boulders, tripping on tree roots and balancing on slippery stones as you criss-cross the stream (which you'll have to do more frequently in winter). If you've brought a picnic, perhaps stop at one of the baker's dozen of waterfalls you pass on this descent — the highlight of the walk, the high main waterfall, is likely to be overrun and noisy.

The SPIRALLING WOODEN STAIR-

CASE (**1h**) shown below eventually drops you down to the bottom of **Richtis Waterfall (❸)** with its pool and picnic table. Time for a shower?

From here to the beach it's about 1.6km or 40 minutes. Although pleasant, the pebbly beach is a bit of an anticlimax after this glorious gorge full of greenery

Left: the 19th-century Lachanas Bridge, where the walk proper begins; below: Richtis Waterfall and the pool below it — a great place to paddle on a hot day.

and birdsong. You may decide to simply retrace your steps from the falls — unless you've come in pairs and left one car at the beach. From the FALLS allow 1h30min back to the start on the main road (⬤), from Richtis Beach allow 2h05min.

Walk 17: FROM ZAKROS TO AGIOS GEORGIOS

Distance: 10.5km/6.5mi; 3h45min
Grade: ● moderate, with a height
difference of 475m/1560ft; mostly
on cobbled trails and tracks; E4
Equipment: walking trainers,
sunhat, water, picnic
Picnic: Zakros Source
Access: 🚌 to/from Sitia (Timetables 6, 8); journey time 1h45min.
Change to 🚌 to Zakros (Timetable
11); journey time 1h10min. Or 🚗
to/from Zakros; park near the village
square (on the main road, with
pharmacy and cafés galore;
35° 6.769'N, 26° 13.149'E)

T his is a particularly pleasant stretch of the E4 which mostly
follows an old donkey trail as opposed to dirt tracks. And
another advantage is that many walkers make for Zakros in any
case, to 'do' the gorge, so this excursion just puts some icing on
the cake — especially for those who stay overnight in Kato
Zakros.

Start the walk in the VILLAGE
SQUARE in **Zakros** (⭕), where the
bus stops: follow the main road
south towards Kato Zakros. After
only 70m, turn right up steps by a
sign for 'E4, TRADITIONAL WATER
MILL, ZAKROS SOURCE'. When you
come to a T-junction with a
FOUNTAIN ahead, it's worth making
a short detour 50m/yd detour to
the right to the attractive and
informative **Water Mill Museum**
(❶). Otherwise keep heading left
along an alley/tarred lane, past a
turning to the right, until you
come to another T-junction after
180m. Turn right here on concrete
for another 180m, when you'll
come to a fork by a large
rectangular WATER TANK on your
right (**15min**). We will turn left
uphill here, following the E4 sign
for 'SKALIA'. But first turn right and
then immediately left, to make a
(half kilometre return) detour to
the small white CHAPEL of **Afendis
Christos** (with beautiful carvings).
Just 200m further on is the
Zakros Source (❷), set in a deep
ravine. This area has been
refurbished with EU grants and
there is seating — a lovely picnic
spot, shown overleaf.
     Returning to the fork, now
make for 'SKALIA', going through a
gate. Then, almost immediately,
head head half-right on a dirt track
which zigzags up past a WATER
TANK after rounding the first
hairpin bend. There's a nice view
down to Zakros from here. From
the tank we follow an ancient
stone-laid trail for an hour as we
ascend about 400m/1300ft.
Although there are some E4
marker posts, there are no route-
finding problems on this very clear
and beautifully preserved trail.
     The way levels out briefly on a
plateau called **Mavrokambos**
(520m; **1h25min**). There's a
feeling of wide-open spaciousness
here, and for a short time you can
just stride out. At a signposted fork
where you can see a farmhouse and
Mt Vigla to the left, keep ahead
along the E4, now on a FARM
TRACK (❸). The greenery of the
cultivation here makes a very
pleasant change from the barren
landscape earlier on. Some 10-12
minutes from the fork (600m),
beyond a gate, turn left on a path
with E4 waymarks — a continua-
tion of the old trail. It skirts to the
left of another PLATEAU and then
climbs to the chapel of **Agios
Georgios** (❹; **2h10min**). You
look up to the ruins of the
abandoned hamlet of **Skalia**.
There's a MEMORIAL here to its
people massacred by the Turks in

105

the 18th century — betrayed by their parish priest! Nearby is a gushing SPRING.

The E4 passes the spring here at the chapel and heads on towards Ziros, but we leave along the dirt road. Coming to a fork after 500m, continue straight ahead over a pass. At the next fork, 400m further on, bear right towards a rocky ridge. But before reaching the ridge, our track bears right,

with lovely views over the Mavrokambos plain. Once down on the plateau and past the farm, retrace your route along the donkey trail and back to **Zakros** (◯; **3h45min**).

Above: the Water Museum at Zakros (open daily except Mondays from 11.00-18.00) and picnic area near the source. Below: the plateau in spring, with its church and nearby spring with water collection pit.

WALK 18: ZAKROS • VALLEY OF THE DEAD • KATO ZAKROS

See also photos on page 107
Distance: 6.3km/3.9mi; 2h15min
Grade: ● straightforward gorge walking, with a descent of 220m/720ft
Equipment: walking trainers, sunhat, water, picnic, long trousers, swimming things
Picnic: anywhere in the gorge or as for Walk 17 on page 105
Access: 🚌 to Sitia (Timetables 6, 8); journey time 1h45min. Change to 🚌 to Zakros (Timetable 11); journey time 1h10min. Or 🚗 to Zakros (park as for Walk 17, page 105). Return on 🚌 from Kato Zakros to Zakros (if you left a car there) or Sitia (Timetable 11), then 🚌 to Agios Nikolaos (Timetables 6, 8); journey times as above

Alternative walks
1 Valley of the Dead (3.5km/2.2mi; 1h); ● a descent of 160m/525ft. Start at the top of the gorge itself, rather than in Zakros. Access and return as main walk, but stay on the bus beyond Zakros and alight by a brown sign, 'ZAKROS GORGE' at a BUS SHELTER in a large SIGNPOSTED PARKING AREA (❼), just before a major bend to the right. By 🚗, park in Kato Zakros (35° 5.820'N, 26° 15.786'E) and take a bus to the start, or park at the head of the signposted gorge and take the bus back to your car. Descend the signed track

from the parking area. When it turns left in a few minutes, go straight on. A steep, step-like section involves negotiation by backside, before you meet the MAIN GORGE (**3**) 10 minutes downhill. Turn right and follow the main walk from (**3**).

2 Zakros — Valley of the Dead — Zakros (13.5km/8.4mi; 4h25min), ● moderate, with a height difference of 220m/720ft. Make a circuit by returning to Zakros on foot: from **Kato Zakros** (**6**) walk back past the PALACE EXCAVATIONS (**5**) to the FORD (**4**). From there follow the 'Old Road' — a zigzagging concreted track, later unsurfaced, past a VIEWPOINT and up to the main road, which you meet at the large PARKING AREA (**7**) where Alternative walk 1 begins. Keep to the main road for 600m, then pick up the 'Old Road' (*Kali Strata*) again — now tarred. Follow it to the 25MIN-POINT in the outgoing route (**1**), then retrace steps to **Zakros** (**O**).

This walk through the Valley of the Dead (Faragi Nekron) is one of our favourites. You can either start in the village of Zakros or from the top of the gorge (Alternative walk 1). Starting from Zakros, you get the benefit of a pretty village and some lush gardens, vines, vegetables, olives and flowers. Not only is the walk splendid, but the goal, Kato Zakros, is a real haven (once the lunchtime coach parties have moved on), with the bonus of a Minoan site. Plan to stay the night if there's room.

Start out in the VILLAGE SQUARE in **Zakros** (**O**): approaching from the north, Kato Zakros is signposted to the right on the main road, but you want to turn *left* towards the church (its two crosses are visible from here). Walk towards the church on a narrow village street, past houses. After just 40m/yds, at a Y-fork, there is a sign left to the 'GORGE', and the E4 goes left. We prefer to go *right* here, towards the church, but either way is fine: both forks meet up later. If you go right, fork right again when you get to the church and follow the village street downhill. Continue by crossing a WATER

CHANNEL. Just ahead, there's a BRIDGE with a glorious splash of bougainvillaea on its left side, and sploshing water invites a bottle refill — even though you are just at the start of the walk! When you come to crossroads a little over 200m from the church, turn right and walk on past the houses, leaving the village on a narrow road (**10min**). Follow this for just under 1km, eventually with a stream bed to your left. Then take the SIGNPOSTED TRACK that leads off left through olive trees (**1**; **25min**). After 130m, at a narrow Y-fork, keep right on the main track. (All these twists and

Left: the walk is very well waymarked with signs and yellow/black paint — as can be seen on the rock at the bottom of the photo. Above: evening at Kato Zakros

turns are waymarked with arrows (sometimes signs as well). Keep right again, after another 130m, where a minor track goes left. The stream bed is still below on your left — a most attractive plane tree-lined ribbon. After another 170m go left at another Y-fork and ignore a minor track straight ahead almost at once, instead making a U-turn to the left. Now the track runs out just before a FENCE and the route continues as a path. By this time you really feel you're in gorge country, and the path quickly descends to the stream bed.

Now following RED DOT WAY-MARKS, make your way through thickets of pink-flowering oleander and cross the stream for the first time on a CONCRETE FORD. Then the ENTRANCE TO THE GORGE through the **Valley of the Dead** opens up before you. Soon a narrow IRRIGATION CHANNEL (not unlike the one in the Mesonas Gorge, Walk 15) runs alongside the path. Before long the **Xeropotamos Gorge** merges from the left (**2**), and the trail heads right (south), quickly reaching a STONE BENCH and (dry) FOUNTAIN

shaded by plane trees (**1h05min**).

Still heading south, the walls of the gorge then close in somewhat, and various caves in the red-rock escarpment betray the location of some 3500-year-old MINOAN BURIAL CHAMBERS (hence the name of this gorge, *Faragi Nekron* — 'Valley of the Dead'.) After the irrigation channel comes to an abrupt end, note the WAYMARKED PATH (**3**) off to the right: it leads up to a PARKING AREA/BUS SHELTER (**7**) on the main road, where Alternative walk 1 begins.

You pass another DEFUNCT FOUNTAIN and the landscape opens out in front of you. Some 20 minutes later, at the end of the lower gorge, beyond a GATEWAY announcing the entrance to 'DEAD'S GORGE' (for those walking up from Kato Zakros), the trail meets a concreted track at a FORD (**4**). Turn left here, passing the impressive Minoan site of **Kato Zakros**, including the PALACE (**5**). Then continue to the welcoming sea and BUS STOP (**6**) at **Kato Zakros** (**2h15min**).

110

Walk 19: BRAMIANA RESERVOIR

Distance: 8.3km/5.1mi; 2h
Grade: ● easy; height difference of
only 40m/130ft, but *no shade!*
Equipment: trainers, sunhat, picnic,
water
Picnic: Agios Georgios church
Access: 🚗 to/from the dam at the
reservoir, reached from Kalamafka
on the Ierapetra road or from
Ierapetra: turn right off the main
south coast road by a large red-
domed church on the west side of
town (signed to 'Bramiana,
Kalamafka'). Park just north of the
dam by the (closed) wooden
information kiosk (35° 2.135'N,
25° 41.588'E).

Water for Ierapetra's tens of thousands of greenhouses comes from Crete's largest freshwater lake, commissioned in 1986. Since then the Bramiana Reservoir has become an important wetland for migratory and nesting birds, with well over 200 species recorded — including some that had previously disappeared from the island. The water level in the reservoir was dangerously low in 2018, but the storms of 2019 filled it to overflowing, burying even the trees. On our last visit prior to publication of this edition, the water level was still high.

Start the walk at the INFORMATION KIOSK (●) where you parked; it is probably closed due to the lack of further EU financing. Head north along the main road towards Kalamafka. After just 350m/yds, turn right on a track, then — if the water is not too high — turn right again almost immediately on a gravel path beside the lake (●; a FIRST BIRD-

The water level in the reservoir was very high when we last researched this walk.

WATCHING AREA). This is one of just two places where you can easily get to the water's edge, since the entire reservoir is fenced off. It's possible, even if your path is clear to begin, that you will encounter water before the path rejoins the track and you'll have to retrace your steps…

Once back on the track, the walk is simplicity itself: just keep to the track closest to the water. You will pass several greenhouses and the remains of an old water millrace on your left. Stop for a break at the church of **Agios Georgios** (❷; **40min**), a lovely setting, before coming to a SECOND, DERELICT BIRD-WATCHING AREA (❸) with a dilapidated 'hide' and broken picnic tables. All the small information panels are faded or derelict, but it is still a pretty spot where you can get down to the water's edge. From here continue to the dam, cross it, and follow the main road back to your car (⭕; **1h45min**).

You will pass the church of Agios Georgios (here taken from the far side of the lake — where you'll also spot tomatoes that never got to market) … and the derelict hide area.

Walk 20: PEFKI GORGE

Distance: 9km/5.6mi; 2h50min
Grade: ● fairly easy — mainly a descent of about 420m/1375ft — but you must be sure-footed and agile. The ascent to Stavromenos church from Pefki adds 2.8km/1.7mi return (200m/650ft)
Equipment: walking trainers or boots, sunhat, picnic, water
Picnic: Makrigialos beach or church
Access: 🚌 to Ierapetra (Timetable 5); journey time 1h. Change to bus along the south coast to Makrigialos (Ierapetra/ Sitia bus, Timetable 10, or Ierapetra/Makrigialos bus, Timetable 22); journey time 30min. Use the same buses to return. Or 🚗 to/from Makrigialos: park on the seafront parking area (35° 2.340'N, 25° 58.520'E). From Makrigialos take a taxi to Agios Stefanos (or Pefki) to begin.
Shorter walk: Pefki Gorge (5.3km/3.3mi; 2h20min). ●‼ Moderate; a height difference of 200m/650ft; you must be sure-footed and have a

head for heights. Access by 🚗 to/from the gorge trail at Pefki (35° 4.388'N, 25° 59.422'E). Follow the main walk from the start of the gorge trail (**①**) 100m west of the PEFKI VILLAGE SIGN to the waymarked fork 1h15min below Pefki, and turn sharp right on the track for 'PISOKA-MINO' (**⑥**). This soon becomes a cobbled trail and zigzags up the western side of the gorge, then follows the western rim along a precarious edge, secured by railings. You rejoin your outgoing route by the FOUNTAIN (**④**) first passed 25min below Pefki, from where you return to the start at (**①**).

Longer walk: Makrigialos — Agios Stefanos — Pefki — Makrigialos (15km/9.3mi; 4h50min; ● fairly strenuous, with an ascent of about 450m/1475ft to begin). This walk *could* be done as an aerobic circuit from Makrigialos. But it's 7km/4.3mi uphill to Agios Stefanos, sadly all on the road these days.

The Pefki Gorge was used by the villagers to take produce down to the coast, and this walk — now part of the E4 — runs along the top edge of the gorge before descending into it. As you descend, you will see the houses of Aspro Potamos (White River), which the villagers originally built as overnight accommodation. From Pefki you could take a 45-minute detour up to the landmark chapel of Stavromenos high above the village.

Starting from the CHURCH in **Agios Stefanos** (**O**) , follow the signposting towards 'PEFKI'. Once the road has done a long sweep around another, smaller, hilltop church, look up to the left: you will see a chapel in the distance, high above Pefki. After a few more bends in the road (about 10 minutes), the beginnings of the village itself come into sight. Notice, about 100m/yds before you come to the sign denoting the limits of Pefki, a MAP OF THE GORGE and a rough CONCRETE TRACK (**①**) leading off to

the right; this is your onward route. Walk on into **Pefki** (**45min**).

(A good 50m/yds past the first houses of the village shallow steps on the left start the climb to Stavromenos (**⑨**), the church perched high above; there is a sign on the wall of the house at the left of the steps. Since it's exhilarating to know you've made it right to the top, you might like to consider this optional detour: although it's a steep, steady climb, it only takes 25-30 minutes to get there and 20 minutes to return. The well-signposted route heads out of the village, where the track gives way to a path.)

When you are ready to head down the gorge — having explored, or had something to eat, or both, head back out of Pefki the way you came in (towards Agios Stefanos). Two minutes outside the village, look for the CONCRETE TRACK (❶) you passed on your way into Pefki; it goes down sharply to the left about 100m/yds beyond/west of the sign denoting the edge of the village. There should be an E4 INFORMATION BOARD here. Leave the road on this concrete track; it used to be the old mule trail going down to the coast and is marked with red dots and arrows.

Turn left after 100m/yds and then go right almost at once — now on a more recognisable cobbled

donkey trail, after 20m crossing diagonally over a concrete track. The waymarking is good as you make your way downhill through the olive groves. The path becomes wider as it merges with a two-wheeled farm track, and there are fragrant pine trees either side.

As the donkey trail comes down into a more open area (15 minutes from Pefki; **1h05min**), you come upon a shady picnic spot with a WOODEN TABLE, a FOUNTAIN and the ruins of **Milos**, an old WATERMILL (❷). The aqueduct which carried water to the mill is still in fair condition. The farm track splits here, one branch curling round left and going back towards Pefki, the other — your onward route — heading on down to the right, seawards. Follow the track for five minutes, then turn left on a waymarked path by a sign,

'GORGE' (**3**). The gorge walls are visible from here and soon you see the south coast through those walls.

At a fork by another FOUNTAIN (**4**; 25min from Pefki; **1h15min**), a sign points down left into the gorge and straight on to Pisokamino *(the return route for the Shorter walk)*. Head left, down towards the gorge. This narrow path descends steeply into the **Pefki Gorge**, where you eventually cross the stream bed. Now descending the right-hand side of the stream, the going needs a bit more attention. Follow the red waymarks: where you think you will have to jump down boulders, the waymarks will show you a way round them. A modicum of agility is required but, soon, once you have picked your way through the rocks for a few moments, you will come to some railings on the right. From here on the route is easier for a time. You then come to two consecutive sets of METAL STEPS (first 17, then 19). These help you negotiate steep drops in the gorge. (The first set may well still be missing two steps — replaced with stout long poles.) Beyond these steps, you cross the watercourse again.

Emerging from the gorge the path crosses an open hillside. Ten minutes later the path comes down onto track (**5**; 1h 20min from Pefki; **2h10min**). Turn right and descend across the river bed. Head towards the coast and, before long, you will have a panoramic view of the whole coastal area spread out below you. About 300m/yds below the river bed crossing, ignore a waymarked track heading back sharp right to Piskokamino (**6**; 1h15min from Pefki; **2h05min**). *(But turn sharp right here for the Shorter walk.)*

Another 500m/yds further on, keep straight ahead (right) where the E4 WAYMARKED TRACK (**7**) goes left

downhill — unless you want to head for Aspropotamos and the White River Cottages visible in the distance. (Our walk goes straight back to Makrigialos.) Almost immediately, disregard a smaller, lower track on the left and continue on the upper, broader one.

Five minutes later you will meet the tarmac road from Makrigialos to Agios Stefanos. Turn left and 25minutes later you will be back at the MAIN ROAD/BUS STOP (**O**) in low-key **Makrigialos** — heading for a lovely swim and a picnic on the BEACH (**8**) or a pleasant seaside meal in one of the tavernas (2h from Pefki; **2h50min**).

Left: in the Pefki Gorge. Below: while Makrigialos has a wealth of tavernas, it's also a delight to picnic in the churchyard with its table, benches and flowers galore.

Distance: 6.5km/4mi; 1h50min (add 1.2km each way if travelling by bus)

Grade: ● easy, with a height difference of 200m/650ft; add 1km if you walk up into Vrises

Equipment: trainers, sunhat, picnic, water

Picnic: any of the churches

Access: 🚌 towards Iraklion (Timetables 1, 8, 14); ask to be put off for Limnes (journey time about 15min). The bus stops only on the national highway (where you will also pick it up on your return). Travelling from Agios Nikolaos, walk ahead (west) along the highway, then take the first left and the first right, to follow the road into Limnes. Coming from Iraklion, walk back (east) along the highway

and take the first left, then the first right. Once in Limnes, follow the road around past a *cafeneion* under a pergola on your right, then past a shrine and a round stone and slate well. There is now a small road bridge on your left, where the walk starts. 🚗: entering Limnes from the eastern (Agios Nikolaos) end, drive through the village towards Neapolis and park near the small road bridge on the left (35° 14.739'N, 25° 38.182'E), as described above for walkers. Our timings start at this bridge.

Short walk suggestions: End the walk at **Vrises** (🚌 Timetables 25, then 1; 2.5km/1.6mi; 50min); do a circuit from **Houmeriakos** church (🚗 to 35° 14.418'N, 25° 37.790'E; 4.3km/ 2.7mi; 1h20min). Grade/equipment as main walk.

This is a very pleasant, straightforward walk via Houmeriakos, affording a good look at three villages with winding streets and lots of character, and a great view at the top of the climb, from Vrises church.

Start the walk in **Limnes** by crossing the SMALL ROAD BRIDGE (**O**) on the left. There is a WINDMILL/WATER PUMP over to the left. As you cross the bridge, you can see Houmeriakos and Vrises up in the hills in front of you. The lane passes through fields and vegetable patches, with many stone and metal wind pumps, citrus, almond and olive trees, and vines. Before long (after 150m/yds) the route comes to a junction where there is a TAVERNA straight ahead (it's a big one, used for weddings, baptisms and celebrations). Turn left, and then go right immediately.

Reach another junction (**5min**), again with many WATER PUMPS, and carry on almost straight across. The road is flanked by low stone walls. Two minutes later pass a small CHURCH on the right and then,

about 10 minutes later, walk into **Houmeriakos** (**❶**; **15min**). The large village CHURCH is on the left (a lovely pine-shaded picnic spot).

With your back to the wrought iron gates of the church, walk straight ahead along the main village street, passing a large SHRINE on the right. Some 50m further on is the village 'SQUARE', with a telephone box; turn sharp left, up the hill, here. Keep right at the CHURCH WITH AN ARCHED PORTICO and then pass a fresh spring-water FOUNTAIN on the left. Now following a broken concrete track uphill, ignore paths coming in from either side. At a T-JUNCTION (with a high stone wall ahead), turn right and then left uphill, passing a BRICKED-UP ARCHWAY on the left. Wind up through the village, eventually with a good view back to Limnes.

Carry on left uphill and then curve to the right. Soon you have joined a tarred lane and are walking through open countryside, heading for a church you can see up on the right. As you reach the CHURCH (❷; **30min**), turn left at the T-junction (a track is to the right). Vrises comes

Jonnie in mimosa-bound Houmeriakos, when first researching this walk

Above: This tiny church below Vrises is a very good picnic spot with plenty of shade and places to sit. Further on, you walk along the 'olive keepers' track'

into sight. As the road makes the first sharp bend to the left, strike off right on a track and then, almost immediately, take the FOOTPATH (**3**) to the left (quite overgrown when last seen, but with grass, not brambles). It rises to the outskirts of **Vrises**, by a SHRINE (**4**; **45min**).

Turn right here, on a grassy two-wheel track.* Meeting a concrete track, turn right — but first look at

*Or first explore Vrises by rising into the village: the BUS STOP **a** is above, on the main Lasithi road, but the lower village brick-paved road is more attractive and leads to the CHURCH (**b**), FOUNTAIN and VIEWPOINT WITH SEATS.

the pretty CHURCH (**5**) to the left, a lovely picnic spot. Take a peek at the next CHURCH (**6**; off to the right) as well. The track changes to dirt now, and on the descent there are good views to Neapolis with its cathedral, with Nikithianos to the right, backed by red cliffs. Just past a huge pyramidal boulder at the left of the track, turn left on a lesser track — a bit steep and skiddy. You brush past a PYLON (**7**) on your left, beyond which the track widens out and improves. Further down, ignore a track off left through olive groves; keep to this main 'olive keepers' track' which makes a U-turn to the right. Meeting a T-junction with a mini-church SHRINE on the right, turn left, then right to the main (but hardly trafficked) road. Not having found Platipodi worth the detour, we suggest you turn right, directly back to **Houmeriakos** (**1**; **1h35min**). You pass a a café on the right just before the square. Walk on to the CHURCH, then retrace your steps to **Limnes** (**O**; **1h50min**).

Walk 22: LASITHI • TAPES • KRITSA

Map ends on page 56
See also photos on pages 31, 58 and 64
Distance: 18.5km/11.5mi; 6h
Grade: ●: moderate-difficult and long, with an ascent of 200m/650ft and descent of 1000m/3300ft. Some loose scree is crossed; danger of vertigo
Equipment: walking trainers or boots, sunhat, water, picnic, long trousers; walking poles
Picnic: overlooking the plateau (the 25-30min-point in the walk)
Access: 🚌 to Malia (Timetable 1); journey time 30min. Change to Lasithi 🚌 (Timetable 25) and ask to alight at the Skapanis café — a large isolated restaurant/café/souvenir shop; journey time 1h30min. (Check in advance whether the bus is going to Mesa Lasithi; if not, take a bus to Tzermiado and taxi from there to the start of the walk.) From

Skapanis café walk 800m downhill to the start of the walk — a jeep track with a large white arrow signpost for 'KATHARO'. If the driver will not stop at Skapanis, you will have to walk 1.7km uphill from Mesa Lasithi. Return on 🚌 from Kritsa to Agios Nikolaos (Timetable 3); journey time 15min.
Short walk: Tapes to Kritsa (6km/ 3.8mi; 1h50min). ● Fairly easy. Equipment as above. 🚌 to Tapes (not in the timetables): departs Agios Nikolaos 06.30, 14.00 daily *(check!)*; journey time 35min. Follow this walk from the 4h10min-point at ❻ to the end (map page 56).
Alternative walk: Lasithi to Tapes (13km/8mi; 4h05min). ●: Grade/ access as main walk; return by taxi from Tapes (pre-arrange or call from the café). A 🚌 departs Tapes daily at 14.45 *(recheck!)*, if you start *really early!* Follow the walk to Tapes (❻).

A vivid picture will remain in your mind when you've completed this walk: the dramatic beauty and moods of the mountains to the north, overlooking the wild, steep valley of Potami. *Do* try to tackle the *entire* walk — even if you do it in two parts (the Short and Alternative walks). Since the walk starts out at 885m/2900ft, not much climbing is involved. You'll cover a good distance without getting too tired.

As the road starts to dip down to the Lasithi Plateau, look out for the large SKAPANIS EMPORIUM (❍) on the right, in the middle of nowhere and ask to be let off there. Then **start out** by walking downhill, past a large white arrow signpost for jeep safaris: 'KATHARO'. Follow the jeep track up to the left (❶; **8min**). Soon there are excellent views of the Lasithi Plateau (**25-30min**) — lovely for picnicking,but don't expect to see the famous windmills from here; you'll get a better look at windmills from Psychro (Walk 23) or Tzermiado (Walks 24 and 25).

Just before you reach the (cross-

less) church of **Agios Apostoli** (❷; **37min**), take the waymarked grassy trail heading left. If it's the right time of the year, you'll have a blaze of scarlet poppies either side of you. After two minutes the trail narrows considerably, and the landscape to the left is very grey-green, tones that stay with you throughout the walk. On coming to the main track again (just over **45min**), turn left. When the track bends round to the right, keep straight ahead on the stonier route. Within a minute, you rejoin the main track. Ignore the cart track off left to a HUT below, surrounded by rock-strewn hills and the

119

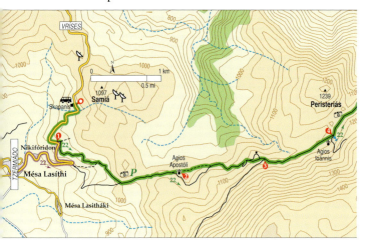

occasional almond tree. Ignore, too, another track rising from the hut a bit further on. When you meet another *TRACK* on a hairpin bend to the right (**❸**; **1h05min**) fork left — straight ahead.

   Pass another small stone *CHURCH* up to your right (**Agios Ioannis**; **❹**; **1h22min**). Keep left just beyond it, passing a stone *WATER TROUGH*. Shortly after that, at a Y-fork, keep right. Soon (**1h30min**) there are magnificent sweeping views to the left. You will be looking over the route the bus took into Mesa Lasithi; it wiggles its way through the valley, with massive mountains forming a dramatic backdrop.

   When the track ends (**1h55min**), a *WAYMARKED PATH* takes you up over the side of the hill ahead. The way is very rocky here; step carefully to avoid the loose rubble. Winter weather and storms can easily damage the path; you may have to cross some rock slides. Then, after a small area of rock-fall, you will have to negotiate a *STRETCH OF SCREE*

From Amigdali (Car tour 7), you have a terrific view of the scree crossed in Walk 22 and of these grey-green mountains.

(**2h10min**). Those who suffer from vertigo might find this section unnerving. If you have a head for heights it's a wonderful place to sit, looking out, with sea in the distance to the right and left!

   Past the scree you will see a short wall — towards which you are heading. But first you'll have to cross a *VERY STEEP DRY RIVER BED* — again, some people may find this part of the walk difficult. Then walk along on top of the *WALL* (**❺**), past a *WATER TROUGH* and a *HUT*. Now the waymarked path leads across an open space carpeted in low shrubs.

There is a stretch where the path disappears; look for PAINT WAYMARKS and head diagonally downhill to join the path. You can see it below — running off to the left over the crest, heading towards Agios Nikolaos. (And, on a clear day, you'll have a lovely, unexpected view of the town itself.) When you approach the far edge of the open area, follow waymarking through a grassy area. Tapes is straight ahead now.

The waymarked route peters out as you come down onto a TRACK (**6**; **3h35min**). Turn left here. The track rounds FOUR SMALL RESERVOIRS and heads down to Tapes. Eight minutes from the reservoirs, and 150, past another small reservoir on the left, you can take a SHORT-CUT TRAIL off right (**7**; **4h**), which will take you more directly down to Tapes. The stony trail gives way to footpath, winding down past a WINNOWING CIRCLE on the left and crossing a stream bed.

You quickly reach the first buildings of **Tapes** (**4h05min**). Walk on past the first group of houses on the left and, just beyond them, fork left downhill. Then turn right. This leads you through the village. A bus

stops here occasionally … just in time to end the Alternative walk.

From here head on downhill, past the CEMETERY WITH CHURCH. After a few minutes' walking on asphalt, you'll come to a *cafeneion* on your right, on the corner of the road where it bends to the left. There is a painted metal spiral stairway on the outside of this cafe (**8**; **4h10min**).

Now referring to the map for Walk 1 on page 56 *(the following numbers are keyed to that map)*, turn off the road and follow the old concrete trail down beside this *cafeneion*. It bends right, and by the last house in the village you come to a T-junction with a wide track: go right for 50m, then turn left on an obvious earthen path heading steeply down into the olive groves in the small valley below. At the bottom of the valley, head right and walk on, going through TWO GATES. After the second gate (within 15 minutes of the olive grove), take the easily-seen old DONKEY TRAIL to the left (**7**). Ten minutes later, at the top of the rise, you can see the sea at Kalo Horio. Follow the rocky path which runs close to a WALL on your right. Within a minute it bends left and through a GATEWAY. Continue downhill on the well-defined route, more or less alongside a wall with a fence on top, and heading in the direction of a LARGE CONCRETE STRUCTURE.

Forty minutes from the olive grove pass a gateway on your right and come onto a TRACK (**6**; 50min

from Tapes; **5h**). Ten minutes later continue straight ahead, ignoring a track going back off to the left. Within half a minute go left at a slanting T-junction. Within another minute pass a STONE BUILDING WITH DOUBLE GATES on your right. Continue straight on, ignoring a track going off to the left (almost directly in line with that track, on the hillside in the distance ahead, is the road going up to the site at Lato). Then, just where the track makes a deep curve to the left, go straight ahead on a DONKEY TRAIL (**4**), keeping the fencing on your right. After two-three minutes follow the donkey trail in a hard bend to the left and then a hard bend back round to the right. Almost immediately the first houses of Kritsa come into view (just over 1h from Tapes; **5h15min**).

When the donkey trail comes down onto a track (1h10min from Tapes; **5h20min**), head right towards Kritsa. Five minutes later you will pass the path leading down right to the KRITSA GORGE (**2**; followed in Walk 2). Turn left, and continue on track towards the village. When you meet the asphalt road from Lato (**1**; 1h20min from Tapes; **5h30min**), turn right over the BRIDGE. The buses turn round and go from a small square up at the far end of the village, so you need to go uphill to the right from the asphalt road. Walk a short way along the road, then turn right up towards the village on a rough track. It narrows and becomes cobbled. When you reach the road that passes through the centre of **Kritsa**, head left downhill again, just past the large church of **Panagia Odigitria**, to where the BUS turns round (**0**; under **6h**).

Walk 23: CROSSING THE LASITHI PLATEAU

See also photos on pages 1,34-35, 123, 129, 138
Distance: 7.3km/4.5mi; 1h35min
Grade: ● easy, almost level
Equipment: trainers, sunhat, water
Picnic: Dikti Cave (shade, rocks to sit on, views to the plateau)
Access: 🚌 to Malia (Timetable 1); journey time 30min. Change to 🚌 to the Dikti Cave (Timetable 25); journey time 1h30min. Or 🚗: park either at the Dikti Cave (35° 9.900'N, 25° 26.869'E) or at Tzermiado (35° 12.079'N, 25° 28.938'E). If you park at the Dikti Cave, take a bus back there from Tzermiado; if you park at Tzermiado, take the Psychro bus to the cave to start (buses *only run Mon, Wed, Fri: recheck times in advance!*). Return on 🚌 from Tzermiado to Malia (Timetable 25), then 🚌 from Malia to Agios Nikolaos (Timetable 1)

Alternatives for motorists: Since this is a short walk, why not use the map to make up your own circuit — or follow the E4 to the Havgas Gorge and back.

Y ou've seen the postcards, now try the walk! It's very straight-forward, along the flat. But remember that despite the many postcards showing whirling windmills, they are used for irrigation, and the sails are unfurled only as required. You won't

The Lasithi Plateau from the road to the Nisimos Plateau and Timios Stavros

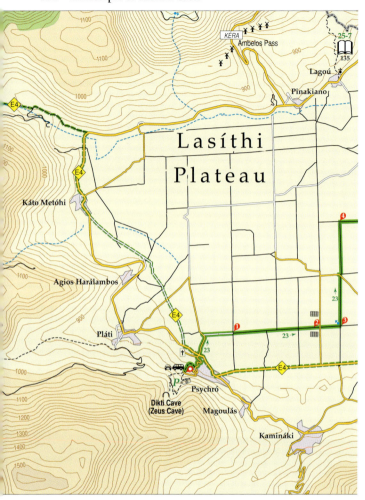

necessarily wander through a myriad of flying sails — although you might be lucky. Even so, you will encounter people at work in the fields, attending to their agricultural round … and yes, adjusting their windmills.

Leave the bus (or your car) in the large PARKING AREA (🅿) above the village of **Psychro**, where all the buses stop. You'll be able to see your destination — Tzermiado — in the distance. Behind it rises a high mountain with a large rounded top, the setting for Walk 24. You'll keep this in view as you cross the plateau. With your back to the paved path that goes up to the DIKTI CAVE (probably the best place for picnicking, with rocks to sit on and plenty of shade), **set off** from the parking area in the corner next to the kiosk, heading due northeast on the

clear downhill path. It merges into crazy-paving-style steps. To your left is the cemetery and church of Plati. From the steps turn down right to the asphalt road that goes up to the parking area for the cave. Head left down the road to the main Psychro/ Kato Metohi road. You'll see a BLUE AND WHITE ROAD SIGN (**5min**), indicating that Agios Nikolaos is to your right and Kato Metohi to the left.

Your tarred track lies ahead, across the road, at the right of the

ceramic workshop and olive oil factory. Immediately you're amongst the cultivation of the **Lasithi Plateau** and will recognise crops of potatoes and courgettes, with scatterings of fruit trees, amongst the chickens and goats. No doubt birdsong will accompany you.

Some 300m/yds along, turn sharp right on another tarred track (**9min**). You cross over a concrete BRIDGE (**11min**), the first of several. There are some sad abandoned

windmills along here. To the right you'll see the village of Psychro. Listen out for the busy encouraging hum of working mills, many of which are power-driven. From time to time, you'll hear goats conversing contentedly, too. Keep straight ahead over an intersection (**14min**), crossing another concrete *BRIDGE* (❶), now following a two-wheeled farm track. Ignore the track leading off left three minutes later — as well as one to the right 150m further on. Have a look at one of the windmills as you pass; it's interesting to see them working. Eight sails is full power here; six or four unfurled is quite common.

When another track heads off to the left (**21min**), ignore it and keep straight ahead. Similarly, keep straight on a minute later, when another track turns off to the right. You'll see the village of Magoulas now, up to your right, on the edge of the plateau. Kaminaki lies just a bit further on, forming another link in the chain of villages on the fringe of the plateau.

Go straight over another intersection (**25min**) and another concrete bridge. Now there's a field of *SOLAR PANELS* (❷) close by on your right and another one on the far side of a field to your left. Keep straight on at the intersection just past the solar panels (**29min**). You may see donkeys tethered, front and back. This gives them plenty of rope — enough to go along the ditch at

The quintessential image of the Lasithi Plateau. It would be nice to picnic here amid the patchwork quilt of market gardens, but finding somewhere to perch is a problem.

and the distinctive mountain peaks behind it lie north-northeast. Cross straight over the next intersection (**36min**) and come to a T-junction with an obliquely crossing tarred track. Turn left, right, left — all this within a few metres.

Before long (**45min**), you'll be just about in the centre of the plateau. Turn right at the next INTERSECTION (**❹**). Soon the track bends to the left and then, a minute or so later, to the right. Follow these bends. Less than five minutes later, you come to a large intersection (**55min**): go straight over. Twenty paces further on, ignore the track coming in from the right; keep straight on the main track.

In another seven or eight minutes (**1h12min**), go straight over another intersection on a very large BRIDGE (**❺**). Keep walking straight ahead along a tree-lined avenue. When you come to an intersection with a round stone structure in the middle (**1h25min**), again go straight over. Cross a wide street in **Tzermiado** and walk another 200m to the MAIN ROAD (**❻**). Turn left, to continue on this main road through Tzermiado. The BUS STOP is just beyond the right-hand turning to Timios Stavros Church, by the ΚΕΝΤΡΟΝ ΥΓΕΙΑΣ (health centre; **❼**; **1h35min**). But if you've left a car at the Dikti Cave, use the map to walk back to it by a different route.

the side of the road, but not enough to let them snaffle the crops either side. Very canny. Depending on the agricultural calendar, you may identify more crops — onions, runner beans, kale, cabbage, wheat. Whatever the crop, the neat cross-channel irrigation system in the fields creates an attractive picture.

At the next intersection, where there are CONCRETE WATER STORAGE TANKS (**❸**) on your left and a fairly tall apple tree on your right (**32min**), turn left. You're now walking due north, and Tzermiado

127

See also photos on pages 1, 123, 126-127, 132 and 134-135
Distance: 20.2km/12.5mi; 6h10min
Grade: ●♦ fairly strenuous because of the distance; possibility of vertigo. No shade. Ascent of 300m/1000ft; descent of 900m/2950ft overall. Be aware that there is a lot of track-walking in the second half, which means the walk can seem like more of a forced march. At least you have wonderful views from the top in mind as you tramp down the tracks!
Equipment: walking trainers, long trousers, sunhat, picnic, water
Picnic: Nisimos Plateau
Access: 🚌 to Malia (Timetable 1); journey time 30min. Change to 🚌

to Tzermiado (Timetable 25); journey time 1h30min. Alight at the KENTPON ΥΓΕΙΑΣ (health centre) in the northwest part of the village. Return on 🚌 from Vrahasi to Agios Nikolaos (Iraklion bus, Timetable 1); journey time about 20min
Short walk: Tzermiado — Nisimos Plateau — Tzermiado (6km/3.8mi; 2h10min). ● Easy ascent/descent of 100m/300ft. 🚌 (Timetable 25) or 🚗 to/from Tzermiado; park at the health centre (35° 12.079'N, 25° 28.938'E). Follow the main walk to the far side of the plain (❷), then return. Or vary your return by using one of the tracks on the map — perhaps going up to Timios Stavros.

T he local people just said 'straight, straight, straight' when we were first trying to find this walk. That's not quite the case, although you certainly have to keep going a fair bit! It's not pioneering, but it is adventurous as walks go — so don't be too exacting about the route — we've simply traced one of *several* possible ways to do this walk. From plateau to plain to mountainside, this route provides great vistas for you. Pick a clear day and you will be staggered by the views over north and south from the highest point in the hike — up where you're unlikely to have the company of anything except eagles and goats.

From the BUS STOP by the KENTPON ΥΓΕΙΑΣ (health centre; ●) at the northwestern edge of **Tzermiado**, **start out** by walking towards the village centre. After a few paces, turn left along a lane (brown signs: 'KARFI MINOAN SETTLEMENT', 'TIMIOS STAVROS CHURCH' and green E4 sign: 'NISIMOS, KARFI'. The lane quickly peters out into a concrete and gravel motor track and leads past a farmyard. Bends take you slowly uphill, far above the Lasithi Plateau. Views improve round every bend.

You pass some ANIMAL PENS (**20min**), where flocks of multi-coloured goats, chickens and sheep may be slaking their thirst at the

water troughs or resting quietly in pastoral peace under the trees. A gentle breeze may be stirring as you climb; look back at the plateau and pick out the working windmills.

Soon you'll notice a band of splendid grey serried rocks, studded with trees and bushes, on your left (**30min**). As the track continues to rise, stone 'portals' frame a tremendous view of the **Nisimos Plateau** and the mountains beyond; the pointed top of Mt Selena (1559m) is straight ahead. This is a lovely setting for a picnic, but there's no shade.

Soon the track forks. The concreted track to the right winds up to the modern church of Agios Timios Stavros with a fine view over the Lasithi Plateau (allow about 1h10min return if you do this on the return from the Short walk). Keep left here, soon meeting a THREE-WAY FORK (**1**). A rusted handwritten sign points left to 'KARFI' (the E4 turns

View over the Lasithi Plateau on the ascent

left here and climbs to Karfi via the chapel of Agia Ariadne; our Walk 25 descends this path). Ignore the two-wheel track in the middle. Our route is the track to the right, which we follow straight ahead, ignoring all other turn-offs left and right. The two-wheel track ends at the FAR SIDE OF THE PLAIN (❷; **1h10min**), where we keep ahead — slightly left — on a clear footpath (*But the Short walk turns back here.*)

Go over a low pile of grey rocks and walk across a small flat area. Look up at the mountains ahead;

you're going towards the lowest dip on the horizon. Climb over another rock pile and join a goats' path, keeping to the right. The path starts to rise; it's surprising how quickly you'll climb, even though the going's not hard — just a steady pull. Remember that you are not heading up to the top of Selena, but skirting round its western flanks.

At a fork (**1h20min**), where there is a rock face ahead of you, go left. In another five minutes you will just be able to see the upper part of Selena. The path becomes less

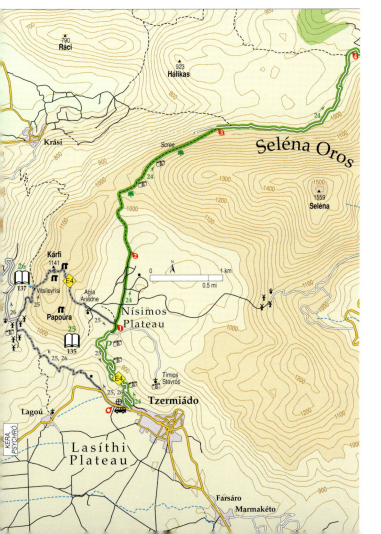

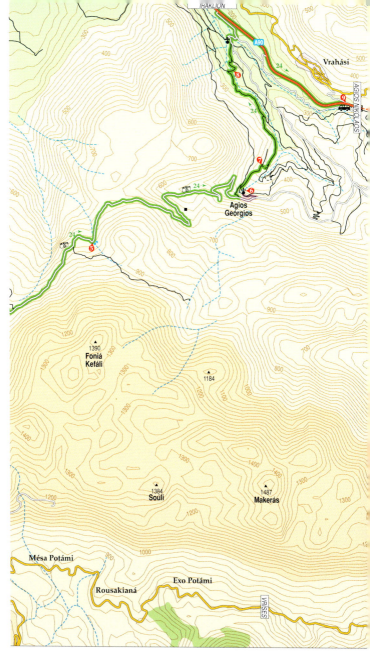

Vrahási

AGIOS NIKOLAOS

Agios
Geórgios

1390
Foniá
Kefáli

1184

1384
Soúli

1487
Makerás

Mésa Potámi

Rousakiá

Exo Potámi

VRISES

discernible as the area you're crossing widens out. Head right, towards a grey stony path and carry on up it, curving round towards the right.

Soon (**1h30min**) Selena should be straight ahead of you. From here there are several goat paths, but keep beside the ridge to your left. The way flattens out, and you can just about make out the route ahead of you, running across the mountain slope. You will see a distinctive, rounded holly oak tree over to your right, in the middle of a miniature 'valley'. Take a rest under its shade. Then climb up this 'valley' and reach a clearing; Selena is right in front of you now. But turn back to face the way you've come: you'll have a fantastic view left, to Lasithi in the distance. To your right you can see Malia and Hersonisos on the north coast. The green basin set just back from the coast is Mohos.

Climb up the shoulder, heading towards Selena. On the ridge to your left you can see a SMALL STONE CONSTRUCTION. Look out for a barely-distinguishable goats' path which traverses the side of the mountain in a northeasterly direction and follow it. The view is breathtaking; you're on top of the world here! Ahead you can see a curved mountain, backed up by a saddle, and then a flat-topped mountain. The path now curves round **Selena**. Doubtless you'll marvel at the view for a while, identifying all the towns and villages

you can spot below. Griffon vultures soar overhead here, keeping watch as you walk on. At this point those who suffer from vertigo may find the path unnerving — there are intermittent stretches where hugging the hillside is difficult. Watch your footing, as the hillside is steep and the path barely trodden.

As you round the mountain, heading northeast (**2h10min**), look out for a SCREE LINE and cross the top of it, keeping slightly uphill. Look carefully to find the path going uphill, and soon you will pass a holly oak tree hanging over the route and providing some pleasant shade. You'll find that the path is leading you gradually downhill, as well as across the mountain, which is dotted with holly oaks. Down to your left you can see the track which you will eventually join.

When the path drops down onto the TRACK (❸; **2h45min**), turn right. After crossing over a COL (❹; **3h25min**), ignore a track curving off to the left (**3h30min**). You can see the way ahead clearly — a pleasant change not to have to watch your step all the time. Now you're

The far side of the Nisimos Plateau, where the track ends and the Short walk turns back

high up over a valley on the left, and the village of Sisi is in the distance on the coast. Ignore a track to your right leading steeply uphill, and shortly after you will come to a CONCRETE WATER CISTERN (**5**; **4h05min**) on your right. Having rounded a bend in the track (**4h25min**), you will pass a fenced-off hut and a CONCRETE REPOSITORY that houses forestry department equipment off to the right. Beyond these landmarks you'll catch your first glimpse of Vrahasi (**4h45min**), set above the Iraklion/Agios Nikolaos road. You can even make out the road tunnel just to the right of Vrahasi.

As you approach the church of **Agios Georgios** below (**6**; **5h**), follow the track in a U-turn to the left.* Then, 250m past the 'U', fork sharp right down to a lower track and follow it to the left. The church is still on your right, on the other side of the valley. You are now walking down the left-hand side of the valley towards Vrahasi.

From here you *could* just refer to the map and choose your own route, but this area is a veritable spider's web of tracks. We suggest: follow this lower, less-used track for just under 500m (four-five minutes). Then, just before it levels out a little

and starts to curve to the left, look carefully for a SMALL PATH (**7**), which curls back down to the right. (The track you are on will end ahead, so you must get down to a track 20m/60ft below.) Zigzag downhill here for two minutes — almost to the floor of the valley — sometimes on path, sometimes on overgrown track. You will then drop down to a more obvious track. Follow it to the left for 800m (just under half a mile), when it makes a tight U-bend to the right. Just at the head of the U-bend, branch off left on another track and follow this one for another 850m, to a T-junction, where you turn right. Ignoring two faint tracks to the left, after 300m you CROSS THE VALLEY (**8**) and come to another T-junction: go left here.

There now follows a series of T-junctions: at the next one (250m further on) go left again. At the following 'T' (after just 100m, past a chapel on your left) go right. At the next (150m further on) go left, walking just to the left of the road. After 400m turn right to the A90 in **Vrahasi** (50min from Agios Georgios; **6h**). Follow the road to the right for ten minutes: a few hundred metres short of the road tunnel, you'll see the dilapidated BUS SHELTER (**O**; **6h10min**).

---

*But to visit Agios Georgios *keep straight on here* for another 100m/yds, *then* bend left to the old monastery. Later, you will return to this junction to continue. The current building dates from the 19th century, although there has been a monastery on this site since Byzantine times. Quite a lot of restoration has been done in the last few years, and a couple of buildings

can be seen as well as the church (don't miss the 14/15th-century frescoes on the north wall or the relief of St George killing the dragon on the south side). Agios Georgios has been a hideout for rebels for centuries (which is why it was twice burnt down), and not surprisingly, it sheltered freedom fighters during World War II.

Walk 25: KARFI CIRCUIT

See also photos on pages 1, 123, 126-127, 132, 136 and 138
Distance: 7.2km/4.5mi; 2h40min
Grade: ● moderate, but with a steep final ascent. Height difference of 300m/1000ft
Equipment: walking trainers or boots, long trousers, sunhat, picnic, water
Picnic: Nisimos Plateau

Access: 🚌 to Malia (Timetable 1); journey time 30min. Change to 🚌 to Tzermiado (Timetable 25); journey time 1h30min. Alight at the ΚΕΝΤΡΟΝ ΥΓΕΙΑΣ (health centre) in the northwest part of the village; same buses to return. Or 🚗 to/from Tzermiado; park by the health centre (35° 12.079'N, 25° 28.938'E).

Another of our walks by the beautiful Lasithi Plateau, this hike climbs to the ancient Minoan settlement of Karfi ('Nail'), then scales the peak of the same name — with brilliant views over the agricultural plain below, mountain chains near and far, and the coast. For the really fit, this walk could be combined with part of Walk 24 or 26 for a really long day out.

From the BUS STOP by the ΚΕΝΤΡΟΝ ΥΓΕΙΑΣ (health centre; **○**) at the northwestern edge of **Tzermiado**, **start out** by walking northwest along the main road towards Malia. After 350m/yds, turn right on a dirt farm track. You pass a large red-roofed FARMHOUSE on the right and then rise through a GATE and set off along the COBBLED DONKEY TRAIL on the far side.

Eventually, after walking for about 2.4km, you come to a track at a SADDLE (**❶**; **50min**) with the sad remains of many derelict WINDMILLS. In the past they ground grains grown on the plateau. Needless to say, the view from here is breath-taking — down to the coast at Malia and even west to Mount Ida, which may well be capped with snow.

Turn right here towards 'KARFI'. You go through another GATE and, at a FORK under 200m further on, keep right (**❷**; **55min**), now heading straight for Karfi. (*Walk 26 turns sharp left at this fork.*) You rise quite easily at this point on a clear trail

through scrub; although narrow, the path is easily seen. You pass a FOUNTAIN WITH A MEMORIAL PLAQUE on the left (**Vitsilovrisi** on the map; **❸**), where a signposted trail heads north to Krasi; bear right here

View west from Timios Stavros to the Karfi summit rising above the Nisimos Plateau

towards Karfi (there may be some RED WAYMARKS to guide you).

From here on the ascent gets steeper … and the waymarks even fainter. These lead us up to another SADDLE and the very scant ruins of the MINOAN SETTLEMENT OF **Karfi**, dating from the 12th century BC. From here a final push brings us to ANOTHER COL and then the TRIG

From the Karfi summit: view to the setting for Walks 26 and 27, with the Aposelemis Dam — the largest in Crete — in the background

POINT PILLAR at the **Karfi** summit (**❹**; 1140m/3740ft; **1h30min**). Take in your surroundings before beginning the descent — and plan your next walks! Just below, to the west is the village of Kera (Walks 26 and 27), while to the east is the Nisimos Plateau and the Selena range which we round on Walk 24; at our feet the patchwork quilt of the Lasithi Plateau (Walk 23).

From the summit drop down 60m/yds to the col just below, then turn left (some *FADED RED WAYMARKS*). The path first heads directly towards the Selena chain, then descends southeast to the **Nisimos Plateau**. When you pass to the left of the **Agia Ariadne** CHAPEL (**❺**; **1h55min**), keep straight on, ignoring turnings both left and right. After 400m you reach a junction on the southern edge of the plateau.

Turn right here: some 150m further on you meet the concreted track to Timios Stavros (**❻**), the chapel on the hilltop to the southeast which has been in sight as you descended from Karfi. It's worth climbing the extra 100m/330ft to the top, for the views. Otherwise, keep straight ahead (past some pleasant picnic spots) and wind down to the main road. Turn left to the BUS STOP or your car by the ΚΕΝΤΡΟΝ ΥΓΕΙΑΣ (health centre) in **Tzermiado** (**Ο**; **2h40min**).

Walk 26: TZERMIADO • KERA • GONIES

See also photos on pages 1, 123, 126-127, 132, 136 and 143
Distance: 12.7km/7.9mi; 3h25min
Grade: ● Straightforward track walking, with an ascent of 150m/ 500ft and descent of about 700m/2300ft
Access: 🚌 to Malia (Timetable 1); journey time 30min. Change to 🚌 to Tzermiado (Timetable 25); journey time 1h30min. Alight at the ΚΕΝΤΡΟΝ ΥΓΕΙΑΣ (health centre) in the northwest part of the village. Return on 🚌 from Gonies to Malia (not in the timetables: departs about

14.30 (Mon, Fri only, Timetable 25), journey time 50min; then 🚌 to Agios Nikolaos (Timetable 1); journey time 30min
Equipment: walking trainers, sunhat, water, picnic
Picnic: Ambelos Gorge
Shorter walk: Kera to Gonies
(8.5km/5.3mi; 2h). ● Grade, equipment and access as main walk, but take the *Lasithi* bus from Malia (Timetable 25) and alight at Kera; journey time 1h. Follow the main walk from the 1h25min-point (**3**) to the end (**8**); return as main walk.

Only recently have walkers been attracted to hiking in the foothills of the Selena range, between the Lasithi Plateau and the north coast. We hope to cater for those of you who want to get away from the 'obvious' landscapes. We suggest two ways of doing this particular walk: Walk 26 is a very pleasant, untrammelled countryside jaunt along tracks — enjoyable for the flora and fauna. Its downside is that you may be unlucky enough to encounter quad bikes. Walk 27 is a truly splendid hike through a gorgeous, steep-sided gorge, high above the river valley. Its downside is that although it is mostly easy, there are a couple of places where the path is extremely steep or narrow and exposed.

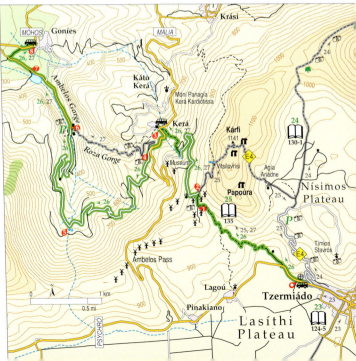

Two of the ruined windmills on the Ambelos Pass

Start the walk in **Tzermiado** at the
Κεντρον Υγειας (health centre; **O**):
follow Walk 25 to the 55MIN-POINT
(**❷**), where that walk keeps right to
head for Karfi. Turn sharp left here,
passing to the right of a *CHAPEL*.
Some 400m further on, ignore a
track off to the left. Then, after
450m, ignore a track to the right.
Instead, make a wide U-bend to the
left and head back the way you've
come, passing a lovely swathe of
greenery and terracing on your right.
Keep to the main track, ignoring a
minor track heading off back to the

right here. Some 80m after passing a
POND on the right, make a tight
hairpin turn to the right on a lesser
track. This peters out into a clear
woodland path which descends to
the main Hersonisos/Tzermiado
road in **Kera** (**❸**; **1h25min**). Turn
left here.

*(If you are doing the Short walk,
the bus will have stopped at the tavernas
just opposite where the path emerges:
head south uphill towards Tzermiado
on the main road to start.)*

Having followed the main road
south uphill for about 380m, you

will come to the second large bend, where there is a break in the roadside barrier. Take the track that goes off downhill to the right here. After just 100m you come to a T-JUNCTION (❹) where you keep straight ahead (left). *(Walk 27 goes sharp right here.)*

Very soon there's a tremendous view of the **Ambelos Valley** into which you will be walking, with the Aposelemis Dam off to the left in the distance. When the track forks some 375m from the T-junction (**1h40min**), keep right, downhill. Keep right again, downhill, under 200m further on. Coming upon WIRE NETTING, keep bending round to the left; don't take any tracks off to the right. Cross over a concrete surface under which there is a water-course going down to the right, and ignore a track running back down to the right; keep straight on.

At the next fork (after 1.2km; **1h55min**), keep right downhill. When you come to a T-junction 600m further on, turn right (**2h05min**). After a splash of aggregate surface you will be back on a rough track almost immediately. A few minutes later, keep straight ahead on the track, ignoring a track going back downhill to the right.

Then (after another 600m; **2h15min**) cross the watercourse (dry in summer). There is an old METAL AND CONCRETE RESERVOIR (❺) in the hillside on the left. Just past this reservoir, if you turn round and look back uphill, you will see the line of old mills — at least 18 in all — that are a landmark up on the Ambelos Pass. Next a stunning plug of rock comes into view just up to the left. Within five minutes, at the next fork, go right downhill. You pass a SHRINE and a LITTLE HOUSE off to the right, on a hairpin bend (650m after crossing the water-course; just over **2h35min**).

Mullein (Verbascum thapsiforme)

Spiny acanthus (Acanthus spinosus)

Field gladiolus (Gladiolus segetum)

Cretan ebony (Ebenus cretica)

Pomegranate (Punica granatum)

Jerusalem sage (Phlomis fruticosa)

Thorny burnet (Sarcopoterium spinosum)

Shrub tobacco (Nicotiana glauca)

As the track bends round to the right and you're almost in the bed of the valley (**2h45min**), look left if you would like to find an old donkey trail which cuts the last main bend off the track. It will be somewhat overgrown in spring so, if you stay on track, continue round the U-bend until you reach the other side of the river valley. The bottom of the valley (**3h05min**) makes perfect grazing ground for flocks, and you will see various animal feeding troughs on the left and pens on the right, hidden in the trees. Stay on the tarmac lane by the river bed, which should be on your left, now.

You are walking the **Ambelos Gorge** — although it doesn't feel like a gorge since the walls are so far apart. Almost at once the **Roza Gorge** (Walk 27) comes in from the right (**❻**), in the setting shown below. You can look up that gorge to the much-photographed modern windmills at the Homo Sapiens Museum. This is just one of several appealing picnic spots in this gorge.

As you come to the end of the valley, near tall telegraph poles, keep left at a wide U-FORK (**❼**; **3h15min**), even though you can just see the first houses of Gonies over to the right by the olive trees. The river bed is still on your left, and you pass a small reservoir with a spillway. Five minutes later, at an intersection, turn right and head towards the village houses. Meet the main road, turn right and walk into **Gonies** (**3h25min**) where there is a super-market, *cafeneion* and petrol station. The BUS (**❽**) stops somewhere near here, wherever it can find a place.

Walk 27: ROZA GORGE

See also photos on pages 1, 123, 126-127, 132, 136 and 138
Distance: 9km/5.6mi; 3h15min
Grade: ●: moderate, with an ascent of 150m/500ft and descent of 700m/2300ft, *but* the path in the gorge demands agility and a head for heights.
Access: 🚐 to Malia (Timetable 1); journey time 30min. Change to 🚐 to Tzermiado (Timetable 25); journey time 1h30min. Alight at the ΚΕΝΤΡΟΝ ΥΓΕΙΑΣ (health centre) in the northwest part of the village. Return on 🚐 from Gonies to Malia (not in the timetables: departs about

14.30 (Mon, Fri only, Timetable 25), journey time 50min, then 🚐 to Agios Nikolaos (Timetable 1); journey time 30min
Equipment: walking boots, sunhat, water, picnic
Picnic: Roza or Ambelos Gorge
Short walk: Kera to Gonies (4.4km/ 2.7mi; 1h50min). ●: Grade as main walk; a descent of 450m/1475ft. Follow the main walk from the 1h25min-point (❸) to the end (❽). Vertigo sufferers might find it easier to walk *uphill* from Gonies: it's less vertiginous but a stiff ascent!

A nother stunning gorge to test your mettle — a real joy for the agile who have a head for heights. As with Walk 15, we suggest that if you have any doubts about your tolerance for heights, you try the *Short walk — in reverse!*

Start the walk in **Tzermiado** at the ΚΕΝΤΡΟΝ ΥΓΕΙΑΣ (health centre; ⬤): follow Walk 25 to the 55MIN-POINT (❷), where that walk keeps right to head for Karfi. Turn sharp left here, passing to the right of a CHAPEL. Some 400m further on, ignore a track off to the left. Then, after 450m, ignore a track to the right. Instead, make a wide U-bend to the left and head back the way you've come, passing a lovely swathe of greenery and terracing on your right. Keep to the main track, ignoring a minor track heading off back to the right here. Some 80m after passing a POND on the right, make a tight hairpin turn to the right on a lesser track. This peters out into a clear woodland path which descends to the main Hersonisos/Tzermiado road in **Kera** (❸; **1h25min**). Turn left here.

Anywhere in the bucolic Ambelos Gorge is pleasant for picnicking, but this spot, where the Roza Gorge tributary joins, is just gorgeous.

141

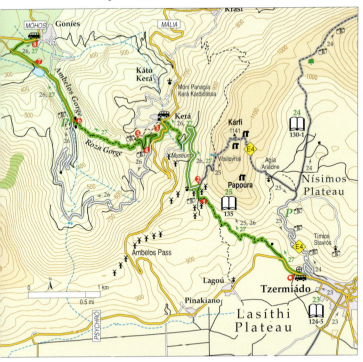

(If you are doing the Short walk, the bus will have stopped at the tavernas just opposite where the path emerges: head south uphill towards Tzermiado on the main road. Otherwise you might ask in one of the tavernas about the path to the gorge which leaves from Kera itself; we've not done it, and it was not signposted at time of checking, but it probably runs off the walkway between the two tavernas.)

Having followed the main road south uphill for about 380m, you will come to the second large bend, where there is a break in the roadside barrier. Take the track that goes off downhill to the right here. After just 100m you come to a T-JUNCTION (❹) where you turn sharp right. The

View north from the start of the walk below Kera. In the background is the Aposelemis Reservoir (also shown in the photo on page 136).

wide dirt track hairpins down, becoming a two-wheeled track through grassy terrain and olive groves before narrowing to a *PATH* (**5**). You are about to start a wonderful adventure: this gorge walk drops almost 400m in just over 2.4km — 1300ft in a mile and a half. The descent starts past a picnic spot with a fine view over Gonies: wooden railings accompany you on this steep descent, but don't lean on them — they are mostly for psychological security! It's almost impossible to believe that this old donkey trail was once the main route between Kera and Gonies: watch your footing on the loose stones.

About halfway along, having overlooked the depths of the green valley, you come into the **Roza Gorge** proper. There are two particularly tricky places — the first a

drop over boulders probably requiring negotiation by backside, the second a very narrow 'airy' passage high above the river, with sheer drops; there are wire railings in place, but again — don't lean on them. The limestone walls of the gorge are most impressive — *roza* means pink, and they may take on that hue in certain light.

Eventually you emerge between two large *ANIMAL PENS* (**6**; **2h40min**) in the setting shown on pages 140-141 and above. You're now in the **Ambelos Gorge**. Pick up *WALK 26* here, just past the 3h05min-point (page 140), to go on to the *BUS* in **Gonies** (**8**; **3h15min**). This is a particularly pleasant part of the walk, with picnic spots galore — almost flat, with pink oleander in the river bed and sheep for company.

Distance: 13.5km/8.4mi; 4h10min. But note that you could also start the walk at Mithi, saving 2km (30min).
Grade: ● strenuous, with some steep climbing up and around three gorges; tight schedule. A good part of the walk follows tracks or roads. Height difference of 400m/1300ft overall
Equipment: walking trainers or boots, sunhat, picnic, water
Picnic: north of Mithi, Metaxohori church
Access: 🚌 to Ierapetra (Timetable

5); journey time under 1h. Then taxi from Ierapetra to Mournies (or Mithi, if you are starting there). Plan to start the walk by 10.45 at the latest, in order to reach Males in time for the only afternoon bus. Return on 🚌 from Males to Ierapetra (not in the timetables): departs 15.30 Mon-Fri only; journey time 40min, then 🚌 to Agios Nikolaos (Timetable 5). If you're pushed for time, the same bus *sometimes* departs Christos for Ierapetra at about 15.20 *(but doesn't always call there; recheck!).*

Three gorges in one walk! Need we say that there are some awesome and breathtaking landscapes on the route from Mournies to Males? It's very obvious that the earth has risen up and writhed about in aeons past, before settling into the dramatic forms you'll see on this walk. The route takes you not only through all this splendid upheaval, but onto the pine-covered hillsides linking four villages strung out across this most attractive pocket of Eastern Crete. You really can't afford to dally on this hike, unfortunately: there's a tight bus connection at the end. Your pace needs to be steady. You must press on. So do not attempt it if you feel fainthearted. Obviously, if you have your own wheels, Walk 29 is the answer.

There are no convenient buses to Mournies, only to Mirtos, 5km away, which has no taxis, so the best option for this walk is to take a taxi from Ierapetra. **Start out** in the VILLAGE SQUARE at **Mournies** (●). From the square keep right on the road to Mithi, ignoring a route up to the left. Quickly leaving Mournies (**5min**), the descending road heads for the hills. Soon (**10min**), when you can see a mountain panorama in front of you, ignore the route bending up to the left. Straight ahead is your destination, Males. Ten minutes later you pass a lovely setting when you're walking through olive trees, with views towards massive mountain folds ahead (**20min**). You can also see the villages of Mithi, in the foreground,

and Males beyond, to the left — looking far closer than it is!

When you come into **Mithi** (**30min**), the CHURCH (❶) is on your right. Just before coming upon a barrage of signposts (100m/yds past the church), turn left uphill on a concrete lane, curving round to the right and rising quite steeply to a group of houses where the way splits into three. Take the central route here. Pass to the left of a CONCRETE WATER TANK and keep left immediately beyond it, rising gently. This track leads you past a small house. Soon you come to a lovely picnic setting under a big tree, with views over the distinctive mountain folds. Later there's another fantastic view down into the deep Sarakina Gorge running back to the Libyan Sea

(**55min**). Just the start of things to come!

From this point, you will keep on this main track for about another 10 minutes, so ignore any smaller tracks leading off it. Having passed a wire fence, you can see a lone, island-like rock rising opposite a deep, impressive gorge (**1h**). The track now appears to be leading you back towards the village; don't worry, it is just taking you past the hill, so keep on following it. The track makes a sharp bend to the left and ends

Fresh-scented pines frame the view over the Sarakina Gorge

150m further on; here start climbing to the right, up a steep narrow path (**1h05min**), which starts beside a small STONE WALL and a WIRE FENCE. (A stone CAIRN *may* be there to show you the way.) Soon, at a clearing, you come to a break in the wire fence: do *not* follow the path ahead, but head left along the fence until you come to a STOCK CONTROL GATE. Go through it and then keep straight ahead. The path now leads you through bright green, fresh-scented pines — via a tributary of the enormous Sarakina Gorge. Huge rocks rear up from inside it; imagine the geological upheaval that created all this splendour.

When you come to the river bed, where the head of this TRIBUTARY GORGE is straight in front of you (**❷**; **1h35min**), cross the river bed and start up the other side on a steep rocky path, from where the views are especially fine. But watch your footing; you may have to step over a small landslide here. Ten minutes later there are fantastic views of the

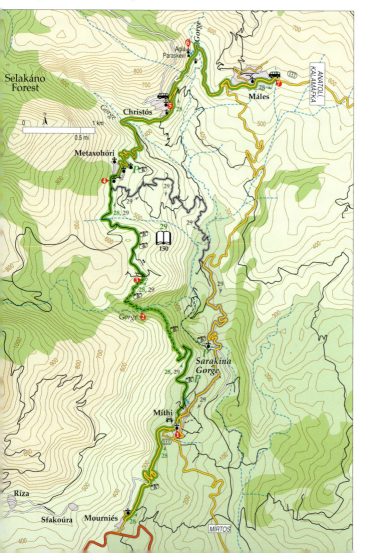

View back to Mournies from the main road during Car tour 8

surrounding country from the far side of a huge boulder at the right of the path. Reaching the top of this climb (**1h45min**), the path levels out. Look to the right again, for more splendid views over the gorge and the hills beyond it, down to the sea. Go straight towards the hill rising in the distance in front of you, bearing in mind that your general direction is Males. The path takes you round the right-hand side of the hill, narrowing and overgrown where vegetation has encroached. You really are off the beaten track! Look out for a STOCK-CONTROL GATE below the hill and go through it, veering to the right of the hill. In places the path is still cobbled, but it's mostly overgrown. At the top of the rise, beyond a small stone wall, walk to the left of a WINNOWING CIRCLE (**❸**), where you will meet a track. Turn right and follow this track (marked with FADED RED DOTS), after only a few paces ignoring a track that leads off abruptly to the right. Before long your track merges with a track rising from an old stone dwelling below to the right, and shortly you will see the first hamlet en route,

Metaxohori, followed by Christos and then Males to the far right. Join a narrow road (**2h25min**) and keep straight on into the ramshackle hamlet of **Metaxohori**. Although a handful of people still live here, there's not much sign of life. The barrel vault roof in the CEMETERY CHAPEL (**❹**) is cracked and dozens of houses are in ruins — all abandoned by people seeking a better way of life on the plains below.

Leave the village on the road hairpinning down to the right; there's an old BYZANTINE CHURCH up to the left and a newer one further down, to the right — its courtyard makes a good viewpoint/picnic spot.

Eventually you reach a first sign announcing **Christos**. This is a very fertile area, with water flowing in off the banks across your road. The contrast between Christos and Metaxohori is marked: although it's also an old and slightly dilapidated village (even the church tower leans over), Christos is definitely thriving. Follow the road in a hairpin bend round to the left, into the village centre (**❺**; **3h10min**). If it's running, you could catch a bus here.

Looking back to Metaxohori on the way to Christos

Then follow the road north out of the village towards Males. Round the bend you'll see a pretty church below in the gorge, and you'll be accompanied by the sound of gurgling water. Soon you can make a pleasant, albeit brief, 'pit stop' at a very quaint taverna. It sits on a raised square, where the very tiny chapel of **Agia Paraskevi** (**6**) nestles beside a huge tree, and a gushing spring is used to cool bottles. Not far past here, the road (still with water pouring down the banks onto it) hairpins round the end of yet another gorge.

As you curve round towards Males (**3h50min**), drink in the views over to the right: you've walked over all those hills almost all the way from the far-distant sea. A little further on, pause again to look down over the remains of a village set below to the right.

You might be tempted by a sign (the back of which you'll see first, on your left) pointing the way back to Mithi down to the right, but we suggest you finish the walk by continuing up the road to Males. On entering the village, curve left up the main road, passing a *cafeneion* and the town hall, both on the right.

Walk to the VILLAGE SIGN at the end of **Males** (**7**; **4h10min**); there are just a couple of houses on the left and an open area where the bus turns round. Here you pick up the *only* return BUS of the day. It could be early, and the bus drivers are not inclined to wait — they don't even turn the engine off. The bus ride back to Agios Nikolaos is wonderfully scenic. Just before the village of Anatoli, another bus waits for the one you're on. It goes on to Ierapetra — in case you're staying in the south.

148

Walk 29: MITHI • METAXOHORI • SARAKINA GORGE (ENTRANCE) • MITHI

See also photos on pages 147, 148
Distance: 13.8km/8.6mi; 4h45min
Grade: ● moderate-strenuous; height difference of 450m/1475ft
Equipment: walking trainers or boots, sunhat, picnic, water
Picnic: Metaxohori church or entrance to the Sarakina Gorge
Access: 🚌 to/from Mithi; park near the church (35° 2.298'N, 25° 34.444'E)

This walk is rather more leisurely than Walk 28 where you have to rush for a bus, and it also takes in the entrance to the spectacular Sarakina Gorge. If you are really fit, you might want to spend some time there.

Referring to the waypoints for Walk 28, **start this circuit** in **Mithi** (❶): follow Walk 28 on page 144 from Mithi to Metaxohori, deducting 30 minutes from all time checks. When you arrive in **Metaxohori** (**1h55min**), pass the CEMETERY CHURCH (❹) and, if you like, perhaps picnic at the BYZANTINE CHURCH (❺) down to the right.

The chapel near the entrance to the Sarakina Gorge is a pleasant picnic spot.

When you are ready to leave, go back to the tumble-down CEMETERY CHURCH (**4**) and retrace your steps for four minutes (250m/yds), then turn sharp left downhill on a track (it's fenced off, but there is a STOCK CONTROL GATE). Follow this track downhill, crossing a cart track after 220m and then ignoring a track off to the right after 250m. After another 250m, at an OBLIQUE T-JUNCTION (**6**), go straight ahead (left) and then turn sharp right 70m further on.

After 130m ignore a faint turn-off to the right, but keep right at a clear fork six-seven minutes later (after 450m). After another eight minutes (700m) turn right at a T-JUNCTION (**7**). Very quickly, ignore tracks to the left, then the right. Two more minor tracks to the right are ignored before you descend to CROSS THE VALLEY FLOOR (**8**; 1h15min from Metaxohori; **3h15min**), lined with reeds and lush plane trees.

Rise up to the MITHI/MALES ROAD and turn right — now you can look across the valley to the route you climbed when you started the walk.

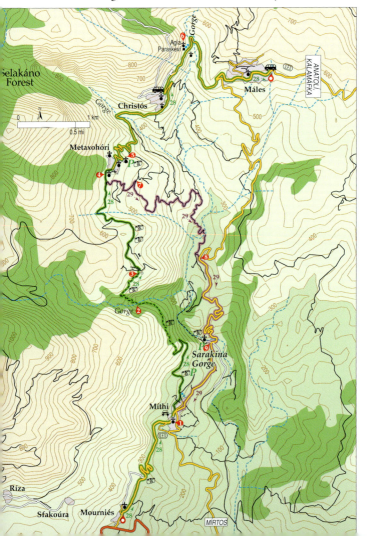

You cross the river bed again in half an hour. Just 100m past the bridge come to the track to the **Sarakina Gorge** (**9**; 2h from Metaxohori; **4h**). This detour (as little as 30 minutes return) is a must! At the left of the dam, take two flights of concrete steps up to a CHAPEL (another nice picnic spot) and a WATER CHANNEL which you can follow short way into the gorge. Or you can spend more time there ... if you aren't pressed ... if the water level permits (it can be waist-high in spring) ... if you have a head for heights and you're very agile (there are high boulders to be clambered over, some with footholds and grips).

Then return to the road and continue on for 15 minutes into **Mithi** to collect your car (**1**; 2h45min from Metaxohori; **4h45min** — *not* including any extra time spent in the Sarakina Gorge).

At the start of the Sarakina Gorge — such a refreshing area, full of water in this thirsty terrain and beautifully edged with cane

Walk 30: PETSOFAS, ROUSOLAKOS AND HIONA BEACH

We suggest two versions of this walk — short and very short! Both explore Minoan sites; they start and finish at the same point and use the same equipment: walking trainers, sunhat, picnic (unless you will be eating at one of the tavernas), water and bathing things. Access is best by 🚗: from the centre of Palekastro (Car tour 2) follow signs for 'Agathis, Chiona, Rousolako'. Park just under 1km along, by a signposted motor track on the right (35° 11.849'N, 26° 16.046'E). Or 🚌 from Sitia to/from Palekastro (enquire locally) and walk there (20 minutes).

Walk a: Petsofas (5km/3mi; 2h).
● Easy, well signposted track and then path; height difference of 250m/820ft. Notes below.

Walk b: Rousolakos and Hiona Beach (3km/1.9mi; 1h). ● Very easy; almost level walking on motor tracks, cart tracks and sand. Notes below.

It's a long haul from a base in or near Agios Nikolaos to the east coast (Car tour 2), and we suspect few 'land-scapers' will be looking for a long walk in this area. So if you make the trip and want to stretch your legs or break the day with a swim, these two short forays are ideal. Walk a visits a Minoan peak sanctuary with few remains; Walk b can explore a fairly well preserved Minoan port town. After either ramble the white sands and clear water of Hiona Beach beckon.

Both walks start from the parking place described above (●): follow the wide motor track signposted 'PETSOFAS', *ignoring* the brown sign pointing left to 'Rousolakkos'. You're walking through a beautiful olive grove — at its best in spring when full of wild flowers. Keep to this wide track, turning right after three-four minutes (250m/yds), then right again after another 100m. After a good 150m, leave this track by turning left (**1**), passing a house. Then, 50m past the house, turn left again at a Y-fork. Just short of 200m further on, the walks split (**2**; **15min**): Walk b turns off to the left.

Walk a keeps straight ahead here, then turns right after another 250m at a signpost for 'PEAK SANCTUARY'. You come to a stock control GATE, walk through a GOAT PEN and leave it some 70m further on via another gate. The path to the sanctuary begins here, marked with a RED DOT (**3**; **30min**).

While the path climbs to the southeast, you enjoy fine views behind you to Kastri and Hiona Beach. Cape Plaka comes into focus, too. It may be barren now, but there are plans to build a huge resort on the cape — running through a road which will impinge on Rousolakos. For the moment the plans are on hold, due to the pandemic and ongoing financial crises.

When the path suddenly veers right, it only takes about 15 more minutes to rise up to the column marking the **Petsofas** SUMMIT (**4**; **1h**). Hang on to your hat! The winds that make these east coast beaches popular with windsurfers are less friendly to walkers.

There are quite a few Minoan peak sanctuaries in Crete, all associated with a nearby settlement area (Rousolakos in this case); our *Western Crete* guide visits Vrissinas, a peak sanctuary above Rethimnon). All archaeologists agree that Minoan peak sanctuaries

were used for religious rituals, and if you visit any of the museums — like Sitia or Iraklion — you'll see pieces of clay figurines that have been found in the environs. But an interesting article we read recently makes a good case for them being also used to supervise agricultural development, especially in newly exploited areas.

Retrace your steps to the start, perhaps not before having a swim in the crystal-clear water, a picnic in the setting below, or a taverna meal.

Walk b leaves the Petsofas trail at (❷; 15min), turning left on a cart track, heading back north — away from Petsofas and towards Kastri, the table-topped mountain shown below. Ignore other cart tracks left and right until, after

Springtime in the olive groves, looking north towards Kastri, the table-topped mountain punctuating the end of the lagoon. Kastri can be climbed — there's a fort on top, built on the remains of an old Minoan fort — but as up on Petsofas, you may be blown away!

This lagoon lies between Hiona Beach and Rousolakos. To the left are no fewer than three tavernas… and Kastri, the table-topped mountain shown on the previous page.

three-four minutes (230m) you meet a wider motor track at an intersection. Turn right here. At a first fork, after 150m, go right; at the Y-fork 50m further on, turn left. Then, after another 50m or so, fork right. **Rousolakos** (❺; **25min**) is now close by on your right. This Minoan town and port (ancient Palekastro) — originally covering more than 50 acres with nine districts separated by a main road — is fairly well preserved… which is more than one can say for the weathered explanatory panels.

After your visit (or not) walk on to the motor track edging the lagoon, turn right and make your way to **Hiona Beach** (❻; **40min**).

Sandy and peaceful, this is nothing like Crete's most popular beaches. There are no umbrellas and no sun beds — although the tavernas may have put out some loungers. The only disadvantage is that it can be very windy. Should you have forgotten your bathing things, just to the southeast is **Bondalaki Beach** — arguably the best in the area, and so private that you could swim in the 'altogether' — people do.

If it's too windy for picnicking on the tamarisk-studded beach, there are three tavernas renowned for their fish dishes. From the one nearest the road, just make your way back to where you parked (**1h**).

Walk 31: SAMARIA GORGE FROM AGIOS NIKOLAOS

Distance (of walk): 18km/ 11.2mi; 4-6h
Open: April/May to October (depending on winter rainfall)
Grade: ● strenuous, particularly if you're not used to walking; the descent is 1250m/4100ft.
Equipment: walking boots or walking trainers, sunhat, water bottle (in which to collect spring water), picnic, swimming things
Access: organised tour (see text below); the price of the ticket includes the boat trip along the coast for your return bus.
Important note: **Do not** try to find a different route to the sea and do not leave the designated path through the gorge. *This is imperative!*

I t's hard to resist the Samaria challenge and, although it's a long and tiring day, it will also be an unforgettable and exhilarating achievement for you! The scenery is spectacular. Don't go down helter-skelter, trying to beat any records; take the walk at a leisurely pace and enjoy the flowers, the birds and the stunning landscape of the Levka Ori ('White Mountains'), as you wander through their depths.

There are frequent excursions to the Samaria Gorge organised by tour operators in Agios Nikolaos and other tourist centres on Crete. (You could also take a hired car to Hania, but that *would* involve an overnight stay.) What a wonderful overview of Cretan landscapes you'll enjoy on this excursion — with two bus journeys and a boat ride to boot!

Your day starts at about 05.00, when you meet your tour bus — at your own hotel or one near your accommodation. (Your day will end at about 23.00.) From the outskirts of Hania, the bus turns south to the

Descending into the Samaria Gorge on the Xiloskala

Omalos (the 'Plain'), where it invariably makes a breakfast stop — thick, creamy yoghurt and Cretan honey. Then there's a further short ride to the top of the gorge, 1220m/4000ft above sea level.

You **start the walk** on the wooden staircase *(xiloskala)*, a staircase built from tree trunks. On your right, the huge wall of grey rock is **Gingilos** Mountain; it rears up menacingly overhead. The staircase becomes a path and drops about 500m/1650ft to the bottom of the upper gorge. There are SPRINGS and DRINKING TROUGHS and a couple of WCs en route. After you pass the small chapel of **Agios Nikolaos**, set amongst pines and cypresses to the right, the route becomes less steep.

At about the halfway mark, you come into the old hamlet of **Samaria**. One of the buildings (into which you can go and sign the visitors' book) has been restored for the wardens who succeeded the original inhabitants when the gorge was designated a national park. This is a popular resting point. From here you'll continue past the church of **Ossia Maria** (the 'Bones of Mary')

and then through the famous 'Iron Gates' (**Sideroportes**), where the gorge is at its narrowest and rock walls soar hundreds of metres above you on either side. Be prepared to take your shoes off here and paddle in the Tarraios River, which is so full in winter that the gorge is closed.

The walk ends where the river meets the sea, at **Agia Roumeli**. You can swim from the beach here before taking your boat to Hora Sfakion, an hour away. The coach will meet you again for the return journey.

After the other walks we've traced out in this book you'll doubtless find Samaria a busy thoroughfare — at times even overcrowded. You certainly won't lose your way either, with all the other people following the same well-worn route. At least you won't have to follow a step by-step set of instructions...

No doubt on the boat trip to Hora Sfakion you will decide to return and explore this area with the help of *Landscapes of Western Crete*. And who knows — you may even introduce some fellow walkers to the pleasures of rambling off the beaten track in *Eastern* Crete.

BUS TIMETABLES

The timetables below represent the basic service; seasonal changes are made in mid-May and mid-September; extra buses run on popular routes in summer. There are usually services from Neapolis to Lasithi as well: enquire about these at your nearest bus station. You can download timetables at www.rethymnon. com/TheBus-Bus-Service-Crete, but they are far from complete, and it's a better bet to collect up-to-date timetables *from the bus station*. See the Index to quickly locate timetable number for each destination; see plans on pages 8-9 for location of bus stations).

BUSES FROM AGIOS NIKOLAOS

1 Agios Nikolaos — Malia — Hersonisos — Iraklion; daily; journey 1h30min
Departs Agios Nikolaos: 06.00*, 07.00*, 07.30, 08.30, 09.30, then hourly at 15min past the hour till 21.15
Departs Iraklion: 06.30*, 07.00, 07.30, 08.15, 09.15*, then hourly at 45min past the hour till 21.45

2 Agios Nikolaos — Elounda; journey 15min
Mondays to Fridays
Departs Agios Nikolaos: 06.45, 09.00, 10.00, 11.00, 13.00, 14.00, 15.00, 17.00, 19.00
Departs Elounda: 07.30, 09.40, 10.20, 11.40, 13.40, 14.20, 15.40, 17.40, 19.20
Saturdays, Sundays and holidays
Departs Agios Nikolaos: 09.00, 11.00, 13.00, 15.00, 17.00, 19.00
Departs Elounda: 09.40, 11.40, 13.40, 15.40, 17.40, 19.20

3 Agios Nikolaos to Mardati and Kritsa; journey 15min
Mondays to Fridays
Departs Agios Nikolaos: 07.00, 11.15, 13.30, 14.30, 16.15, 20.00
Departs Kritsa: 07.30, 11.30, 13.45, 15.00, 16.30, 20.15
Saturdays, Sundays and holidays
Departs Agios Nikolaos: 07.00, 11.15, 13.30, 16.15
Departs Kritsa: 07.30, 11.30, 13.45, 16.45 (16.30 on Sun)

4 Agios Nikolaos — Neapolis — 'Dikti' Cave; journey 1h30min
May only run in summer; check locally!

5 Agios Nikolaos — Istron — Gournia — Ierapetra; daily; journey time 1h
Departs Agios Nikolaos: 06.30*, 07.30**, 08.15, 09.45, 11.15, 13.15, 15.15, 16.15, 18.15, 21.15
Departs Ierapetra: 06.30, 08.30, 10.15, 12.15, 14.15, 16.15, 18.15, 20.15

6 Agios Nikolaos — Kalo Horio —— Istron — Gournia — Sitia; daily; journey time 1h45min
Departs Agios Nikolaos: 06.15*, 08.15, 12.15, 15.15, 20.15
Departs Sitia: 05.30*, 07.00**, 08.30*, 11.30, 14.30, 17.30

7 Agios Nikolaos — Elounda — Plaka; daily; journey 40min
Departs Agios Nikolaos: 09.00, 11.00, 13.00, 15.00, 17.00
Departs Plaka: 09.30, 11.30, 13.30, 15.30, 17.30

BUSES FROM SITIA

8 Sitia to Iraklion via Agios Nikolaos; daily; journey 3h15min
Departs Sitia: 05.30 (07.00 on Sat/Sun), 08.30**, 11.30, 14.30, 17.30
Departs Iraklion: 07.00, 10.45, 13.45, 18.45

9 Sitia — Palekastro; Mon-Fri only; journey 40min
Departs Sitia: 06.00, 11.00, 14.30
Departs Palekastro: 07.30, 11.20 16.00

10 Sitia — Makrigialos — Ierapetra; daily; journey 1h30min
Mondays to Fridays
Departs Sitia: 06.15, 12.40, 14.30, 19.15
Departs Ierapetra: 06.15, 08.30, 09.30, 12.30, 14.30
Saturdays
Departs Sitia: 09.00, 12.40
Departs Ierapetra: 09.30, 12.30
Sundays
Departs Sitia: 12.40
Departs Ierapetra: 09.30

11 Sitia — Palekastro — Kato Zakros; Mon-Fri; journey 1h
Departs Sitia: 06.00, 14.30
Departs Kato Zakros: 07.00, 15.15

BUSES FROM IRAKLION

12 Iraklion — Hersonisos — Malia; daily; journey 1h; from Station A (near the harbour)
Departs Iraklion: from 06.30 to 22.00 half-hourly (every 15min from 08.30 to 11.00 and from 14.00 to 17.30, except Sundays)
Departs Malia: 06.45 and from 07.30 to 23.00 half-hourly (every 15min from 09.30 to 12.30 and from 15.00 to 18.00, except Sundays)

13 Iraklion to Agios Nikolaos; daily; journey 1h30min; from Station A (near the harbour) *See Timetable 1*

14 Iraklion — Agios Nikolaos — Ierapetra; daily; journey 2h30min; from

Station A (near the harbour); journey
time 2h30min
Departs Iraklion: 07.00, 08.15*, 09.45,
11.45, 14.45, 16.45, 19.45
Departs Ierapetra: 06.30, 08.30, 10.15,
12.15*, 14.15, 16.15, 18.15, 20.15

15 Iraklion — Agios Nikolaos —
Gournia — Sitia; daily; journey 3h15min;
from Station A (near the harbour)
See Timetable 8

16 Iraklion — Lasithi Plateau (Diktaion
or 'Dikti' Cave); only Mon and Fri;
journey 2h; from Station A (near the
harbour)
Departs Iraklion: 14.15
Departs Diktaion Cave: 05.45

17 Iraklion to Arhanes; daily; journey
30min; from Station A (near the
harbour)
Mondays to Fridays
Departs Iraklion: 06.30, then hourly on the
hour until 21.00
Departs Arhanes: 07.00, then hourly on the
hour until 21.00
Saturdays/Sundays
Departs Iraklion: 07.15*, 08.00, 09.00*,
11.00*, 13.00, 15.00*, 17.00, 19.00*
Departs Arhanes: 08.00, 09.00*, 10.00*,
12.00*, 14.00, 16.00*, 18.00, 20.00*

18 Iraklion to Agia Pelagia; daily;
journey 35min; from Station A (near the
harbour)
Departs Iraklion: 08.45*, 14.30
Departs Agia Pelagia: 09.40, 15.20

19 Iraklion to Festos; journey 1h30min;
from Station B (outside the Hania Gate)
Mondays to Fridays
Departs Iraklion: 07.30, 09.00, 10.30, 11.30,
12.30, 14.00, 15.30, 16.30
Departs Festos: 10.00, 11.45, 12.30, 14.00,
14.45, 15.30, 17.00, 17.45
Saturdays, Sundays and holidays
Departs Iraklion: 07.30, 09.00, 09.30, 10.30,
11.30, 12.30, 14.00, 15.30, 16.30, 18.00
Departs Festos: 09.45*, 10.30, 11.45*, 12.30,
14.00*, 14.45, 15.30, 17.00, 17.45

20 Iraklion — Mires — Agia Galini;
daily; journey 2h; from Station B
(outside the Hania Gate)
Departs Iraklion: 06.30 (07,30 on Sun),
09.00, 12.45*, 14.00, 16.30
Departs Agia Galini: 07.20*, 09.15, 11.45,
15.00*, 17.00, 19.15

21 Iraklion —Mires — Matala; journey
2h; from Station B (outside the Hania
Gate)
Mondays to Fridays
Departs Iraklion: 07.30, 12.45, 13.00
Departs Matala: 07.00, 09.30, 15.00
Saturdays, Sundays and holidays
Departs Iraklion: 07.30, 09.00*, 11.30,
12.45*, 15.30
Departs Matala: 07.00*, 09.30, 11.30*,
13.30, 15.00*, 17.15

BUSES FROM IERAPETRA
(See also Timetables 5, 14)

22 Ierapetra — Koutsouras —
Makrigialos; journey 30min
Mondays to Fridays
Departs Ierapetra: 06.15, 08.30, 09.30,
12.30, 14.30, 18.30
Departs Makrigialos: 07.00, 08.45, 10.15,
13.15, 15.15, 19.15, 20.00
Saturdays
Departs Ierapetra: 06.15, 09.30, 12.30,
14.30, 18.30
Departs Makrigialos: 07.00, 09.45, 13.15,
15.15, 19.15
Sundays and holidays
Departs Ierapetra: 09.30, 14.30, 18.30
Departs Makrigialos: 13.15, 15.15, 19.15

23 Ierapetra — Xerokampos — Mirtos;
journey time 30min
Mondays to Fridays
Departs Ierapetra: 06.00, 09.30 (only Mon
and Fri), 10.30, 12.30, 14.30, 17.00, 20.00
Departs Mirtos: 07.00, 10.50, 13.15 (12.50
on Tue, Wed, Thu), 14.50, 17.20, 20.20
Saturdays
Departs Ierapetra: 08.00, 12.30
Departs Mirtos: 08.20, 12.50
Sundays and holidays: no service

24 Ierapetra — Viannos — Iraklion;
journey 2h30min
Mondays and Fridays only
Departs Ierapetra: 05.45, 17.00
Departs Iraklion: 09.30, 15.00

BUS FROM MALIA
(See also Timetables 1, 12)

25 Malia — Hersonisos — Lasithi
Plateau (Diktaion or 'Dikti' Cave); daily
in summer only *(recheck locally!)*; journey
1h30min
Departs Malia: 08.00 (Sun), 09.00*
Departs Dikti Cave: 14.00*, 15.00 (Sun)

Index

Geographical names are the only entries in this index. For other entries, see Contents, page 3. A page number in *italic type* indicates a map; a page number in **bold type** indicates a photograph. Both of these may be in addition to a text reference on the same page. 'TT' means Bus Timetable number; note that the numbers following TT are *timetable numbers*, not page numbers. The Bus Timetables are on pages 157-158. Pronunciation: the syllable to be stressed is indicated by ´ (for example: Anatolí/Anatolee).